SAFE MONEY
in
TOUGH TIMES

EVERYTHING YOU NEED
TO KNOW TO SURVIVE
THE FINANCIAL CRISIS

JONATHAN D. POND

New York Chicago San Francisco
Lisbon London Madrid Mexico City Milan
New Delhi San Juan Seoul Singapore
Sydney Toronto

The McGraw·Hill Companies

1 2 3 4 5 6 7 8 9 0 DOC/DOC 0 3 2 1 0 9

MHID   0-07-162961-0
ISBN   978-0-07-162961-4

This publication is designed to provide accurate and authoritative information in regard to the subject matter covered. It is sold with the understanding that neither the author nor the publisher is engaged in rendering legal, accounting, or other professional service. If legal advice or other expert assistance is required, the services of a competent professional person should be sought.

> —From a Declaration of Principles jointly adopted
> by a Committee of the American Bar
> Association and a Committee of Publisher

McGraw-Hill books are available at special quantity discounts to use as premiums and sales promotions, or for use in corporate training programs. To contact a representative please visit the Contact Us pages at www.mhprofessional.com.

This book is printed on acid-free paper.

Contents

PART V
Planning for a Secure Financial Future

Preface

I n spite of how helpless you feel riding the economic roller coaster, you can overcome the fear and confusion of the Great Recession. There's no more critical time than now to stop letting your money control you so that you can control your money. *Safe Money in Tough Times* will help you make sense out of the often conflicting and always confusing opinions of "experts" about what you should be doing with your investments and other personal financial matters during these challenging times. Unlike other authors and commentators, I will not tell you to put all your money into gold or canned goods or to hide your money in a mattress. I'm also not predicting a depression, but I think we are going to have to endure a formidable and lengthy recession with a slow recovery, clearly the worst worldwide economic crisis since the Great Depression.

If you're looking for something bizarre to do with your money, you've come to the wrong book. What I will show you is how to invest wisely and well amidst downright scary investment markets, using investments that you already understand. But there is a lot more involved in surviving the Great Recession than investing. I will help you if and when you become a victim of the slow economy—if you lose your job or fear that you may lose your job, if you get into debt problems, or if you're having trouble affording college tuition for your children. An entire section of the book, "Tackling Special Situations," addresses the problems that will befall many people over the next couple of years. The Internet can be a useful resource for guidance and information to help you improve your financial status. The Appendix contains a list of helpful financial Web sites.

Tough financial times need not be a totally negative experience, however. Because our financial lives are unsettled during an uncertain economy, we are forced to take a closer look at the way we manage and spend our money. This will not be a bad time to begin to discard some bad financial habits and replace them with better habits. As hard as it may be to believe in light of the stock market and economic meltdowns, there are many opportunities to grow financially during an awful economy, and these opportunities will be discussed in the chapters that follow. I hope you will find a lot of useful information in this book so that you can approach the challenges ahead with more confidence and, in the process, be able to sleep a little bit better, knowing that you are back on the road to achieving financial security.

SPECIAL READER WEB SITE

The economy and investment markets will undoubtedly change frequently as we struggle with the worldwide economic crisis and emerge from the doldrums. The special reader Web site will keep you up to date on changing conditions and provide further guidance on keeping your money safe in tough times. Check it out from time to time: www.jonathanpond.com/safemoney.html.

ACKNOWLEDGMENTS

This book has benefited immensely from the assistance of several very capable people. The encouragement and helpful comments of Jeanne Glasser, my editor at McGraw-Hill, are much appreciated. Ruth Mannino handled the production process with great skill. The assistance of my associates, John Annino, Joan Lohr, and Richard Merrill, is gratefully acknowledged. Financial authors Alan Lavine and Gail Liberman offered many useful suggestions, as did my agent, Peter Ginsberg. I sincerely appreciate the efforts of all of you.

By now my wife, Lois, and our three daughters, Elizabeth, Laura, and Emily, are accustomed to the inevitable long absences that are endemic to book authoring. But it is no less stressful, and I thank them once again for their forbearance.

Part I

Understanding the Economic Crisis

1 WHAT'S GOING ON IN THE ECONOMY?

What's going to happen to me?

There's no doubt about it: these are tough times for Americans—indeed, for families throughout the world. *Safe Money in Tough Times* will help you and your family deal with the challenges. Whatever problems the bad economy dishes out to you, you will find help in these pages. How bad are things? In just one day in late 2008, the following events were in the news:

- Stocks drop another 4 percent; they're down almost 40 percent so far this year.
- Seventeen major retail chains may be in jeopardy.
- Small business owner optimism index is at a multidecade low.
- Bailout plans strain as a growing number of companies need assistance.
- Circuit City files for bankruptcy.

- U.S. auto manufacturers are on the brink of bankruptcy; General Motors stock is at a 66-year low, with some analysts predicting that the stock price will go to zero.
- Orbitz lays off 10 percent of its workforce.
- American Express gets access to bailout money, as a rising number of cardholders are having trouble making payments.
- Economists predict that the recession will be one of the longest in history.
- Starbucks' profit tumbles 97 percent.
- Leading home builder reports that customer traffic and sales hit record lows.
- AIG reports a huge loss; rescue package is raised to $150 billion.
- Worldwide economic crisis worsens; China announces $586 billion stimulus package.
- A survey of large businesses reveals that none planned to hire over the next three months.
- DHL announces 9,500 jobs to be cut.
- 280,000 homes entered foreclosure in the previous month.

What's going on with the economy? And more importantly, what does it mean to you? How will you and your family be affected? What should you do now to protect yourself from the tough times ahead? Some people have been severely affected by the worldwide economic crisis. What if you're one of them? This book will help you understand what's going on and, more importantly, will show you what you can do to survive the economic doldrums, no matter how badly you are affected. What's more, *Safe Money in Tough Times* will show you ways to take control over and manage your finances in such a way that you'll emerge from the Great Recession well positioned to prosper during better economic times.

HOW WE GOT INTO THIS MESS

There is a lot of blame to go around for the global financial meltdown. A conglomeration of factors converged to make a perfect storm. The complex problems hit a crescendo when banks found themselves unable to make loans.

Many people blame lax financial regulation and consumers who, along with the U.S. government, borrowed like there was no tomorrow. Then there were the lenders who carelessly made loans to borrowers with poor credit. Of course, investors who failed to research their investments and Wall Street firms that engaged in excessive risk taking share the guilt. Add in securities rating agencies that overrated risky securities and credit-scoring companies that allowed human beings to be removed from much of the lending decision-making process. It was a recipe for disaster.

Thirty Years in the Making

The seeds of the financial meltdown may have been planted as far back as the 1970s under the Carter administration. The economy was stagnating, and taxes were high. Many people believed that deregulation of the financial industry would result in more private investment in stocks and bonds and spur economic growth. It also would allow U.S. financial institutions to better compete globally.

At the same time, government policies focused on homeownership and small business, which many considered the keys to building economic prosperity. The Community Reinvestment Act of 1977 required commercial banks and savings institutions to make loans in low- and moderate-income neighborhoods. Subsequent administrations, both Democratic and Republican, built on these programs, which eventually led to the unraveling of the economy.

The Federal Housing Enterprises Financial Safety and Soundness Act of 1992 required two secondary mortgage market players to support affordable housing. The government-sponsored players were the Federal National Mortgage Association, or "Fannie Mae," and the Federal Home Loan Mortgage Corp., or "Freddie Mac." This action led to the proliferation of riskier no- and low-down-payment mortgages.

Subsequently, the Clinton administration encouraged home loans in the nation's inner cities and rural areas. The Financial Services Modernization Act of 1999 repealed the Glass-Steagall Act of 1933, which prevented banks from engaging in investment banking and vice versa. As a result, banks began getting into the securities business in a big way—and vice versa.

The bursting of the technology and dot.com bubble at the turn of the century was followed by an extended period of low interest rates and skyrocketing home prices. An industry of third-party mortgage brokers blossomed, with limited regulation or accountability.

The combination of these political initiatives fueled widespread aggressive lending and relaxed standards for home loans, and encouraged speculation. Competition among several types of lenders led to loans with increasingly low monthly payments and no income documentation. Unfortunately, these lower-payment "option" loans were often riskier and more costly than traditional 30-year fixed-rate mortgage. Yet, those loans increasingly were made at higher interest rates to lower-income borrowers. Many people who ordinarily would not qualify for a mortgage were issued home loans.

A Double Whammy

The straw that broke the camel's back came in 2007, when interest rates rose and home prices fell. The U.S. government put Fannie Mae and Freddie Mac into conservatorship in the last half of 2008 because they were nearing bankruptcy. Making matters worse, mortgages had been packaged by Fannie Mae and Freddie Mac and sold to investors. Borrowers often did not know who actually owned their loans. In addition, quasi-insurance contracts transferring the risk of the mortgages to others had also been sold, with little regulation or oversight. Today, the big question has become how to value those "credit default swaps" and other so-called credit derivatives created from mortgage pools. The disaster started in the United States but quickly spread overseas.

The government will move to stimulate the economy under the Obama administration. Rebate checks or tax cuts will be given to lower- and middle-income Americans in an attempt to prop up the sagging economy. Massive job creation programs will also be undertaken. Efforts by leading banks and the U.S. government will help stem foreclosures.

This debacle will eventually begin to subside. But even then, individuals and families will probably spend years getting out from under the adverse effects of the Great Recession.

A GUIDE FOR SURVIVING THE GREAT RECESSION

Now that you have some understanding of how we got into this mess, it's time to begin to consider what actions you need to take, both to survive the downturn and to emerge from it in sound financial condition so that you can take advantage of the prosperity that always follows recessions. After showing you why we're not headed for a depression, despite some irresponsible talk about it in the media, Chapter 3 provides some information on things you can do right away to minimize the effect of the recession on your finances. The remainder of the book is divided into four sections: "Coping with Tough Economic Times," "Investing in Tough Economic Times," "Tackling Special Situations," and "Planning for a Secure Financial Future." Since the Internet can be a wonderful resource for guidance and software to help you deal with your financial challenges, I have listed my favorite financial Web sites in the Appendix.

Parts II and III will guide you through a variety of concerns as you try to grapple with your personal finances, including saving, managing your debt, budgeting, reducing expenses, maintaining your insurance, and, of course, investing wisely and well after the terrible drubbing that investors have suffered.

Part IV deals with special situations that may be of concern. In fact, it is quite likely that a few of these special situations will apply to you and your family. They include coping with unemployment, working through credit problems, challenges for homeowners, and helping your family survive the psychological problems that often accompany distressed family finances. This section also includes tips for worried preretirees and retirees, paying for college in tough times, and survival strategies for small business owners.

The last section of the book will provide some advice to help you recover from the effects of the economic tsunami so that you can prosper in the next economic boom. It also takes a look at how the new administration may affect your pocketbook.

Finally, my special *Safe Money in Tough Times* reader Web site will keep you up to date on matters affecting the economy and your financial well-being. The address is www.jonathanpond.com/safemoney.html.

When all is said and done, financial security is what personal financial planning is all about. Unfortunately, we are going through a period of time that may interrupt a lot of people's progress toward achieving their financial aspirations. I hope that after reading the pages that follow and taking appropriate action, you will be able to look back at this time as an annoying, but not overwhelming, disruption in your personal financial progress, one that helped you prepare for an even better financial future.

2 THIS TIME IT'S DIFFERENT, BUT WE'RE NOT HEADED FOR A DEPRESSION

The scary word *depression* has been popping up on the airwaves, but don't let it rattle you. A depression is a severe decline in economic activity that lasts for years. Economists already acknowledge that we are in the midst of a recession, which is a temporary but significant decline in economic activity. In fact, many have called this country's economic state the worst recession since the Great Depression of the 1930s.

THE GREAT RECESSION

Although the recession is likely to turn out to be severe, economists have stopped short of calling it a depression, even though that may be how you feel when you open up your monthly investment statements. Why? The U.S. government takes a much more active role in the economy than it did during the Great Depression of the 1930s.

Today we have safety nets, like federal deposit insurance, social security, unemployment benefits, and welfare programs. If the situation gets particularly dire, the government can step in and lower interest rates, or even take over institutions or companies. We've already been watching this happen in the government bailouts of Fannie Mae, Freddie Mac, AIG, and Citigroup, with more names to be added to the list.

You might think that residential real estate is one sector of the economy that is experiencing problems similar to those in the Great Depression. New housing starts have dropped 64 percent since their peak in 2006. That sounds like a lot. It's certainly similar to the decline during the 1974 recession. But in the 1930s, housing starts dropped a whopping 90 percent.

As in the Great Depression, unemployment is rising. It could hit 8 percent or more, based on estimates. But that, too, is a far cry from the 1930s, when about one of every three persons was out of work.

Fortunately, we are benefiting from low inflation, running at around 2½ percent. That's mild even when compared with the double-digit inflation rates of the 1970s. During the early part of the 1930s, there was a 20 percent annual *deflation* rate. That means that prices dropped 20 percent annually because no one had any money to spend or save.

Economists acknowledge that we could see economic growth decline further. But they expect nothing like the gross domestic product decline of 26 percent that occurred during the period from 1926 to 1932.

LESSONS LEARNED

Even if things do get worse, we have already learned many hard lessons, and we are better prepared to deal with crises in the economy and the investment markets. In the wake of the 1929 stock market crash, the Federal Reserve was too slow to lower interest rates and stimulate the economy, and there was no federal deposit insurance. Thousands of bank failures resulted. This time around, the Federal Reserve and the U.S. Treasury have already acted to keep the financial crisis from spreading. They're on the lookout for ways to pump money into the economy and help companies and homeowners. In fact, we even saw global unity, with several countries taking economic action simultaneously.

There's no denying that we're in a mess. For years, both businesses and consumers borrowed from Peter to pay Paul. Banks made low-rate adjustable-rate mortgages to persons who could not afford the homes they bought. Meanwhile, banks packaged these loans into securities and sold them to institutional investors. The institutional investors purchased credit default swaps to protect themselves against losses from mortgage defaults.

The end result: homes went into foreclosure, and banks and investors in mortgage-backed securities and credit default swaps lost their shirts. The real estate bubble burst, interest rates rose, and housing values plummeted. It became impossible to place a value on certain investments, and insurance companies were unable to cover losses.

Unlike what happened in the Great Depression, however, our government came up with an initial $700 billion to bail out our financial system. Lenders started modifying mortgages to avert foreclosures. Some beleaguered homeowners were able to make lower, more affordable monthly payments. In addition to financial institutions, other struggling companies lined up for government largesse.

Other major differences between now and the Great Depression: some corporations, such as Microsoft, are maintaining low debt levels and still have tons of cash on the books. And on the employment side, there are still a lot of people earning money and, hopefully, saving it.

No one knows for sure exactly how much it will take to get us out of this mess. Does all this mean that Uncle Sam is buying consumers and businesses a free lunch? Heck, no! Uncle Sam is borrowing more money. Our country's budget deficit will be in the trillions of dollars. Future generations, unfortunately, will pay for our mistakes. I can only hope that everyone — individuals, families, businesses, and governments — will learn a lasting lesson.

Is Deflation on the Horizon?

Falling prices for consumer goods are one of the few welcome by-products of the steep decline in economic activity. Fuel, transportation, clothing, and housing costs declined in late 2008, and if the price declines continue, there is at least some risk that the economy will go through a period of deflation.

But before you jump for joy at the specter of everything becoming cheaper, deflation can have a very serious impact on an economy. Borrowers, banks, and businesses would all be hurt by deflation, as happened during the Great Depression of the 1930s. As prices fall, consumers and businesses become less willing to spend and invest. After all, why buy something now if it will be cheaper next year? Businesses would be compelled to reduce prices further to attract buyers, thrusting the economy into a downward spiral. Sustained deflation will shrink the economy, and unemployment will rise.

Any family or business or government that is in debt can be hammered by deflation as well. Borrowers benefit from inflation because they pay off their loans with "cheaper dollars," money that has less purchasing power. But under deflation, the purchasing power of money actually increases, which means that borrowers are paying back their loans with money that has *increased* in real value. It's the equivalent of having to pay back a $1,000 loan with $1,100 plus interest.

While deflation is still very unlikely, if trends suggest that it is a possibility, here are some defensive measures you can take:

- Put more money into short-term bond funds and money market funds.
- Buy dividend-paying stocks of companies that will be able to cope with deflation.
- Pay off as much debt as you can.
- Put off any large purchases.
- Enhance your job skills so that you can stay employed in the event that unemployment skyrockets.

3 Checklist of Things to Do Now to Get Your Financial Act Together

*I remember past recessions. We had a real tough time—
we almost lost the house. We're in better financial shape
now, but I still worry about what's going to happen, since
the economy is going to take a long time to get back on
track. I want to be prepared this time.*

Tough economic times affect us all; unfortunately, some people suffer more than others. Don't wait for recession problems to affect your personal finances any more than they already have. You can do a number of things today to prepare for the troubles that may lie ahead. The rest of this book will describe these important matters in more depth and help you address problems that may be affecting you now or in the near future, such as investing when most people are scared of the stock market, family money problems, and unemployment. The following checklists can help you begin to organize your financial life so that you will not be taken by surprise if and when a financial problem arises during this long and severe recession. It's never too late to prepare.

Budgeting and Record Keeping

- Prepare a household budget that lists past and expected future income and expenses. Through this budget, you can identify spending patterns and adjust them, if necessary, to reflect changes in your financial situation or outlook. If you're not into budgeting, accomplish the same objective of improving your financial position by increasing your savings through automatic transfer from your paycheck or bank account into an investment or savings account. (See Chapter 5.)

- Evaluate your sources of income and how you spend your money so that you can plan ways to reduce expenses or earn extra income should the need arise. (See Chapter 6.)
- Prepare a summary of your assets (home, investments, and so on) and liabilities (debts) so that you can get an idea of what you own and what you owe. This summary will help you identify what resources you have available to meet future obligations.
- Organize your personal records so that you have ready access to important family documents and personal financial information. If you need to address a pressing financial problem, the last thing you'll want to have to spend your time on is locating and organizing your records.

INSURANCE

You don't want to risk an expensive uninsured loss in the midst of a weak economy. Review your insurance policies to make sure you have adequate, but not excessive, coverage in the following areas. (See Chapter 8.)

- Health insurance
- Disability insurance
- Homeowner's or renter's insurance

- Automobile insurance
- Extended personal liability (umbrella) insurance
- Professional liability insurance if you have your own business
- Life insurance

Long-term care insurance may also come in handy later on if you or a spouse or partner needs home health care or nursing home care.

DEBT MANAGEMENT

- Summarize your loans and other obligations, including payment schedules, so that you can plan to meet these obligations comfortably. (See Chapter 7.)
- You are entitled to receive a free credit report annually from each of the three credit bureaus: Equifax, TransUnion, and Experian. To request your reports, visit www.annualcreditreport.com or call (877) 322-8228. Don't respond to ads for "free" credit reports that end up costing you money. Review your credit reports for accuracy. If you find any errors, request that they be corrected.
- Review your loan status to determine your capacity to increase your borrowing should you need to.
- Reevaluate any contemplated major purchases, such as a home, home improvements, or an automobile, in light of the current economic situation. While the economy may benefit from these purchases, it may make sense to postpone them. (You can rely on other members of your community to boost the economy by buying things they neither need nor can afford.)

INVESTING

Summarize your investments so that you can

- Ensure that they are appropriate in light of current and expected economic and market conditions. (See Part III.)
- Make sure that they are adequately diversified. (See Chapters 9 and 10.)
- Determine which investments you could cash in easily to meet emergency financial needs, if necessary.
- Determine whether you have sufficient ready resources to meet three to six months' living expenses in the event of a financial emergency. (See Chapter 14.)
- Keep abreast of current conditions in the financial markets as the economy struggles through the recession so that you or your investment advisor can monitor your portfolio effectively and make appropriate investment changes.

TAX PLANNING

- Familiarize yourself with tax-saving techniques so that you can increase your income by minimizing your income taxes.
- Keep abreast of possible changes in tax regulations under the new administration that may necessitate changes in your investment and tax strategies. (See Chapter 31.)

RETIREMENT PLANNING

- Adding to your investments regularly is the surest way to build up your wealth, so continue contributing to your retirement plans [IRAs, 401(k) plans, and so on].

- Prepare a retirement projection to identify any changes you may need to make in order to be able to retire comfortably. (See Chapter 24.)

Planning for Retirement

- Evaluate how rising living costs and declining investment markets will affect you over the next two years.
- If your investments are already well diversified, avoid making any large changes in them.
- Don't hesitate to seek the advice of family members or trustworthy professionals about your financial challenges.

Other Matters

- If you have children who are in or about to enter college, review your plans for meeting the costs and, if necessary, seek alternative ways to pay for college. (See Chapter 23.)
- If you have aging parents, encourage them to consult with you if they have any financial concerns as a result of the deteriorating economy. (See Chapter 25.)

If you devote some time to reviewing these matters, you will be in a much better position to deal with present or future problems relating to the long and deep economic crisis. In addition, your financial situation will be on track to thrive when the economy begins to improve.

PART II

Coping with Tough Economic Times

---

4 TWELVE WINNING STRATEGIES TO COPE WITH TOUGH TIMES

People in my community are really beginning to feel the effects of the economic decline. There was a layoff down at the plant. Sometimes I feel like we're just biding our time before something bad happens to us. I wish there was something we could do to prepare, but I haven't the faintest idea where to begin.

There are a lot of things that you can and should do to protect yourself and your family from many of the financial problems that have already arisen and are likely to continue to plague us in the future. Some problems are probably beyond your control, like the loss of your job, reduced income, and investment setbacks. Others, however, can be avoided by realistic planning and perhaps some sacrifice. The dozen strategies that follow will help you take better control of your financial future, so that you can avoid the avoidable and survive the unavoidable. The chapters that follow discuss these strategies in more detail.

1. Build Up Your Savings

One of the most important things you can do to protect yourself from the financial adversity that will strike so many people during this recession is to build a cushion of savings to fall back on. In late 2008, the ranks of the unemployed were swelling by over 50,000 *per week*. Millions of additional workers may have their salaries frozen or even cut. Nothing can beat money in the bank (or in an accessible investment account) to help you shoulder these burdens, should they arise.

Another benefit of setting aside emergency funds is that you'll worry a lot less about what's going to happen to you and your family. If you've already been putting money aside regularly, that's great. If you're particularly concerned about your financial well-being over the next year or so, you may want to increase your savings rate a bit. If you haven't been saving up to this point, it isn't too late to start. In fact, it is crucial that you begin to set aside some money—even a few dollars a week is better than nothing. For additional information about building up your savings, see Chapter 6.

2. Get Your Debts under Control

Millions of people are choking on consumer debt. They're sitting on a house of cards—the slightest disruption in their personal financial situation, and they may be headed for big trouble. Whatever your debt situation, take the necessary steps to get your debts under control, particularly credit card loans. First, don't add to your indebtedness. If necessary, take the scissors to all but one of your credit cards. Second, keep up to date on all of your obligations, and third, work to reduce your debts if they are excessive, even if it means putting your spending on a crash diet.

People with excessive debt have an awful lot to lose if they are victimized by the Great Recession. People whose debts are under control may suffer a minor setback or two, but they will emerge relatively unscathed and well prepared to take advantage of better economic times. Chapter 7 provides guidance on getting your debts under control.

If you feel you can't afford to both save and whittle down your debts at the same time, try doing a little of both, even if it may take you more time to pay off your loans. Having some money set aside to help you cope with any future financial problems will help you sleep better at night, even though you may not be putting as much toward your debts as you would like. When times get better, you can better afford to increase your debt payments.

3. Maintain Your Good Credit

Whether you have a lot of debt, a little debt, or no debt, you need to maintain a good credit rating so that you can access credit if you need it during the tough times. Dipping into savings is preferable to incurring debt if your income drops or if you have to meet unexpected expenses. But your circumstances may dictate that you have to borrow temporarily to make ends meet. Don't let poor credit make your life even more difficult. Chapters 7 and 19 will help you maintain or restore your good credit standing.

4. Maintain Your Insurance Coverage

Unfortunately, many people reduce or eliminate essential insurance coverage when they are confronted with a family money crisis. It may seem to be a relatively painless thing to do at the time. For example, they may drop their renter's insurance or they may decide to go without health insurance if they are laid off, rather than pay high premiums to maintain the coverage.

The problem with leaving even a single gap in your insurance coverage is that it exposes you to a possible uninsured loss, which could end up jeopardizing not only the assets that you currently own but also some of your future income as you struggle to rebuild after a big drain on your assets. Chapter 8 discusses ways to ensure that you have adequate insurance as well as ways to reduce your insurance expenses.

5. Remember that It's Your Money

The helpless feeling accompanying scary investment markets causes many investors to rely too much on the opinions of others, more so than they would under more stable economic conditions. Investors who were managing perfectly well during normal markets end up in disarray during more turbulent markets.

While the opinions and advice of others may be helpful, remember that it's your money, even if someone else is managing it for you. Be particularly wary of anyone who thinks that he can predict the near-term future of the investment markets. Such people are delusional and should be encouraged to seek immediate counsel from a mental health professional. The more you understand what you're investing in and keep current on market conditions, the better you will be able to preserve your money now and grow your money once again when the investment markets rebound, which they will.

6. Continue Saving for Retirement

After suffering devastating losses in their retirement savings plans at work, many people are reducing or eliminating their contributions. After all, they argue, why throw good money after bad? But they're wrong. The only sure way to increase your retirement savings is to make regular contributions and regularly increase the amount that you're contributing. If you're worried about losing money on your next contribution, put it in a low-risk money market fund or stable value fund choice that is available through your plan.

7. Keep a Diversified Portfolio

There is nothing like a bear market to cause investors to become preoccupied with short-term market performance. Of course it's no fun watching your portfolio decline in value, but periodic investment losses are both inevitable and unpredictable. It is essential to avoid investing in extremes during a recession—liking stocks one week, loving bonds the next week, hating them both the next month. For more information on how to diversify your investments, see Chapter 9.

8. Select High-Quality Investments

Don't make investments that don't make sense. Many people like to gamble with their investment money, hoping to recoup their past losses by selecting speculative stocks or investing in high-interest bonds. Certainly some people can afford to speculate a little, but all too often they end up losing even more money on securities that are too risky. The worldwide economic crisis has already devastated the prices of stocks, particularly speculative stocks. If the recession deepens, the devastation will continue. You should favor high-quality securities or mutual funds that invest in them. High-quality investments are much more likely to survive, if not thrive, in the worst economic circumstances. Weed lower-quality investments out of your portfolio now. Chapters 11 through 14 will guide you in selecting high-quality stocks, bonds, real estate, and temporary investments, respectively.

9. Anticipate Any Contingencies

Don't deceive yourself during this recession. You need to review your current situation regularly, so that you can anticipate any problems before they occur. These problems could include the loss of your job, salary freezes or reductions, credit problems, unexpected expenses, or problems managing your investments. Uncertain times call for careful evaluation and planning; the sooner you anticipate a problem, the more time you have to address it. Part IV contains several chapters that can assist you in anticipating and addressing problems that frequently occur during tough economic times.

10. Get Help if Adversity Strikes

Millions of people have already been hurt financially by this enormous and long-lasting recession. Many will be reluctant to get the help that is available to assist them through trying times. Family financial problems often require tough choices. But making tough choices is certainly preferable to letting the situation deteriorate even further. Several chapters of this book provide sources of assistance for financial problems that you may encounter in the areas of insurance (Chapter 8), job loss (Chapter 15), debt problems (Chapter 19), mortgage problems (Chapter 20), problems meeting tuition costs (Chapter 23), problems of small business owners (Chapter 26), and bankruptcy (Chapter 28). Finally, remember the support that family members and close friends can provide during trying times (see Chapter 27).

11. DON'T DWELL ON THE NEGATIVE

It's easy to look at the worldwide economic meltdown as a serious and perhaps lifelong setback in your financial life. At best, people think that their financial lives have been seriously impaired, and the media, always delighting in reporting the worst, are eager to reinforce your negative thoughts. Indeed, everything you see, read, or hear about the outlook for both working-age people and retirees is nothing but pessimistic. But dwelling on the negative serves no purpose other than to increase your angst and diminish your sleep. The economy will recover, and if you're well positioned to benefit from the recovery, you'll eventually look back at the Great Recession as a minor annoyance. But in order to do so, you have to have a positive attitude.

12. BE A SURVIVOR

You *can* survive whatever adversity this recession throws your way. You probably have some acquaintances who have gone through tough times in the past and are doing just fine now.

Many people have survived the sudden loss of their jobs, and many more will in the future. They don't stay unemployed forever, and they often end up with better jobs. Many people have lost their homes through foreclosure, and many more will in the near future. Most of them will be homeowners once again, and own a nicer home. Most people have suffered major financial losses as a result of plummeting worldwide stock markets. But most investors will enjoy the rebound in stocks with greater investment savvy and a larger portfolio. No matter how bad things are, you will be a survivor.

5 BUDGETING FOR TOUGH ECONOMIC TIMES

My paycheck just seems to disappear. I try to spend less, but it seems that as soon as I get my head above water, new bills roll in. How can I begin to save in order to provide a cushion if something bad happens to my finances?

It's always hard to save money, but as times get tougher, your expenses may grow faster than your income, or your income may drop. It gets harder and harder to make ends meet, let alone put anything away for the future. Almost everyone's saving and spending habits can be improved, but before you can change anything, you must take a look at where your income goes, so that you can identify areas where you can cut back. Businesses can't plan their spending without a budget. The best way for you to keep track of your spending so that you can control it is to prepare a budget, much like a budget that a business would prepare. A plethora of Web sites is available that offer fill-in-the-blanks budget worksheets, and some of my favorites are listed in the appendix. On the other hand, if you, like most people, abhor the notion of budgeting, there are other, less labor-intensive ways to reduce your spending. This chapter will emphasize a stream-lined approach to reining in household expenses.

BUDGETING WITHOUT THE BUDGET

Budgeting can be a useful exercise, but most people have nei-ther the time nor the inclination to prepare a household budget. The purpose of a budget is to motivate you to live beneath your means, so that you spend less than you earn. This is particularly important if you are concerned about your financial future amidst the economic woes and you want to build up a cushion for any tough times that may arise. Of course, even a well-prepared budget is of no use unless you are prepared to live within its strictures. But there is another way to spend less than you earn without going through the drudgery of budgeting. All you need is a retirement, brokerage, or savings account.

- **Workplace retirement savings plans.** If your employer offers a retirement savings plan, like a 401(k) or a 403(b), then by all means start there. If your employer offers a match, so much the better, but even if it doesn't, contributions to these plans are, in effect, tax deductible.
- **Regular contributions to an IRA account.** After contributions to workplace plans, transferring money into an IRA account (and, if you have income from self-employment, a self-employed retirement plan) is next in

order of priority. Your brokerage or mutual fund company will be happy to hit up your checking account every month and put the money into your IRA account. That's a lot easier than trying to come up with a few thousand dollars to fund an IRA contribution all at once.

- **Plain old savings.** Last but not least, with your instructions, any financial or investment institution will also automatically withdraw some money from your checking account or, if allowable, your paycheck and place it in an investment or savings account. Putting money into a savings account has one advantage over putting it in retirement accounts: you can withdraw the money for a financial emergency without, in the case of a workplace retirement plan, the hassle of borrowing from the plan or, in the case of an IRA, having to pay taxes and perhaps a penalty.

Whichever way you slice it, automatic investing is a great way to both begin and stick with a regular savings program that can stand you in good stead if times get tougher. I refer to automatic investing as "better living through electronics," since the money you're setting aside for the future is electronically transferred from your paycheck or bank account. The money is thereby removed from any financial temptations that might arise. The result is relatively painless budgeting. Since you never get your hands on the money, you shouldn't miss it, particularly if you start small and gradually increase the amount that's transferred.

Quick and Dirty Expense Saver

The following table shortcuts the budgeting process by simply listing expense categories that you and other family members may be able to reduce, and in some instances eliminate if push comes to shove. Ideally, you will first list the approximate amount you're now spending in the left column. But that isn't essential. You can go directly to the right column and put in the amounts that you think you can reduce. You should be surprised at how much you can cut back without depriving yourself too much. Let's face it, life has been sweet for the several years preceding the economic tsunami. Bad spending habits were cultivated, and they can be curtailed without undue pain.

Candidates for Spending Reduction

	Current Spending Level	Amount You Can Reduce
Food, alcohol, tobacco	$_____	$_____
Restaurants	_____	_____
Household maintenance	_____	_____
Furnishings, equipment	_____	_____
Clothing	_____	_____
Transportation	_____	_____
Medicine, medical/ dental care	_____	_____
Personal care, grooming	_____	_____
Education	_____	_____
Recreation	_____	_____
Contributions, donations	_____	_____
Gifts	_____	_____
Laundry, dry cleaning	_____	_____
Total	$_____	$_____

Making It Work

Anyone who has ever tried to lose weight knows that no matter what menu you draw up, you won't get any thinner until you diet. Putting your spending on a diet works the same way. No matter how much fat you cut out of your budget, you won't see any results unless you can keep your actual spending just as lean. Set reasonable spending limits, and leave a comfortable margin for unexpected expenses. If you can stick with your plan to reduce expenses, you'll have at least one less thing to worry about as you endure the current economic meltdown and prepare to thrive in the future. Having even a small amount of money set aside in an emergency fund or investment account could be the difference between being a victim of the recession and being a survivor.

Safe Money Checklist

Budgeting to Protect against Rough Times Ahead

✔ The best way to save is to save regularly and automatically.
✔ Examine your spending to identify areas where you can cut back.
✔ The key to success is sticking with your expense reduction plan.

6   WHAT TO DO WHEN YOUR EXPENSES ARE INCREASING FASTER THAN YOUR INCOME

I just got a notice at work today that there will be no raises this year because business is down. My wife's company has asked management to take a 10 percent pay cut. We are really feeling squeezed. Our utilities, taxes, and car operating costs are rising by leaps and bounds, but our pay isn't. We are already dipping into savings to meet our living expenses, and it looks like our situation is going to get worse.

Millions of American workers have to endure steadily rising living expenses even though their pay is not being increased or may, in fact, be being reduced, particularly if they lose a job and have to take a new job at lower pay. It is painful to see the prices of many necessities going through the roof when your take-home pay seems to be moving in the opposite direction. Even if you are lucky enough not to suffer any major financial disruption during this challenging economic environment, you still may have difficulty making ends meet. If you find yourself fearing that your income may be frozen or simply won't keep pace with the rising costs of living, the next sections will help you minimize the discomfort, including a dozen relatively painless ways to reduce your expenses and a half-dozen ways to get some needed extra cash.

CLOSING THE GAP BETWEEN INCOME AND OUTGO

If your income isn't going to rise in the foreseeable future, or if it isn't rising as much as your expenses, there are actions you can take to maintain a sound financial footing. No one knows how long this crisis will last, but if you heed some of the following suggestions, you will be prepared to weather the worst of it. Also refer to Chapter 5, which offers guidance on budgeting.

- **Put your living expenses on a diet.** Although you may not want to think about it, reducing your living expenses is the best way to make ends meet when your expenses are creeping up faster than your income. At this point you probably are saying, "There's no way that I can reduce my expenses." If that's what you think, you haven't thought hard enough.

- **Reduce your savings rate.** Another way to increase the amount of cash that you have available to meet living expenses is to temporarily reduce the amount that you save. If you have been a regular saver up to this point, you will probably be pained by the notion of reducing your savings rate, and will restore it to its former level as soon as you can. Unless your situation is particularly precarious, try to continue saving at least a small amount each week or month. This will give you a psychological boost during an otherwise stressful time, and those added savings can provide a cushion if the economic doldrums continue or worsen.

- **Find other sources of income.** In addition to or rather than putting your expenses on a diet, you can close your fiscal deficit by fattening up your income. You may want to consider moonlighting or, if you are a homemaker, taking a part-time job to enhance household revenue.

- **Dip into savings.** Although dipping into savings to meet living expenses is a painful action to take, some people will have to do so in order to cope with strains on their family finances. This action should be taken *only* after you have thoroughly and realistically examined better alternatives for weathering the storm, such as reducing your living expenses and finding other sources of income, as described previously.

- **Borrow.** Borrowing to meet living expenses is a last resort. One general rule of thumb for individuals, businesses, and, I hasten to add, governments is that you should never borrow to meet current expenses. Just look at the federal government and the many states and cities that have borrowed to balance their budgets, only to end up in dire financial straits. Nevertheless, if you already have reduced your living expenses to the bare necessities and taken other actions such as those discussed earlier, you may need to borrow to avert financial disaster. Don't assume that you can just go out and get a loan, however. You may not qualify for a loan under your present circumstances, not to mention the reluctance of lenders to do much lending at all. Even if you can, you may end up spending years extricating yourself from your indebtedness, much like the government.

Case Study—John and Natalie

The Dilemma

John and Natalie fear that they are in for some tough financial sledding. John just got word that he isn't going to get a raise this year, and his employer indicated that if business conditions don't turn around quickly, all employees may be required to take one week of unpaid vacation. Natalie works as a part-time real estate agent, and the local real estate market stinks. She thinks that her income will be down 40 percent next year, if she's lucky. Fortunately, John and Natalie see the handwriting on the wall and are already hard at work figuring out what they are going to do over the next 12 months to address the problem that millions of other families face: declining income and increasing living expenses.

Their Plan

John and Natalie know that their income is going to decline by at least $8,000 next year, and they estimate that inflation alone will increase their living expenses by $5,000. In sum, they have a total negative change in their finances for next year of an unlucky $13,000, assuming that there are no major changes in their lifestyle. Since they have anticipated these problems, they are taking action to minimize them. To avoid making matters worse, they have wisely decided to forgo any big-ticket purchases next year that would add to their expenses. For example, they wanted to trade in their five-year-old car next year for a new one, but now they agree that they can put up with the old car for one more year. (In your author's opinion, they can put up with a five-year-old car for another five years, but I digress.)

Even if they postpone any big purchases, how are they going to balance the books? After a lot of studying—and some disagreement on the details—John and Natalie have decided on the following actions.

1. They will reduce their living expenses by $7,000 next year by taking a less expensive vacation, dining out less fre-

quently, taking their morning coffee and lunch to work rather than buying it, and becoming more budget conscious.

2. They are reluctantly reducing their savings level from $200 to $120 per week. This is particularly painful because the savings are earmarked to help pay tuition for their two young children, but under the circumstances, they are glad they won't have to eliminate all their savings. This will close the budget gap by another $4,000.

3. Finally, they are going to dip into their savings accounts for the additional $2,000 necessary to balance their income and expenses. Of course, they could have accomplished the same thing by reducing their savings by another $40 per week, but they need the $2,000 immediately to pay their holiday and winter heating bills.

Borrow from Your IRA if You Need a Short-Term Loan

If you need some extra money fast, you can borrow from your traditional IRA account once each year per account. As long as you redeposit the money in one of your IRA accounts within 60 days, no penalties or taxes are assessed. This once-per-year privilege applies to each IRA account if you have more than one. So if you have multiple IRA accounts, you could make a withdrawal more than once a year. But be careful. If you don't replenish your IRA within the 60-day limit, you'll pay taxes on the distribution and, unless you're over age 59½, the withdrawal will also probably fall victim to a 10 percent penalty.

A Dozen Ways to Reduce Expenses

Most people are already feeling pinched financially, and it is likely to get worse before it gets better. Many of us will have to cut back in order to build up a financial cushion to weather the storm that is ahead. Others will have to cut back on expenses just to make ends meet. Here are a dozen ways to reduce your expenses.

1. **Brown-bag it at work.** This doesn't mean that you should bring alcohol to work in a plain bag, although the way the economy is going, you may be tempted to. Instead, start bringing your lunch to work. Have you ever calculated how much you spend on lunch at work over the course of a year? It's probably the equivalent of one month's rent or mortgage payment. Sure, the cafeteria manager or local deli is not going to appreciate my telling you this, but I'm more concerned that you survive this recession and achieve financial security. Bringing your lunch can be a major step in that direction.

2. **Buy generic.** It makes good sense and saves a lot of cents to buy generic prescription drugs and over-the-counter medicines. If you want to save even more, order them by mail. But don't stop there. You probably think that generic groceries are inherently inferior. Have you tried them? You can always go back to wasting your money on more expensive brands if your taste buds are offended.

3. **Appeal your property tax assessment.** Surprisingly, a large percentage of people who appeal their property tax assessments end up with a lower bill. Don't forget, property values have already dropped in many areas of the

country and will drop in many more as the recession continues.

4. **Leave the car at home and use public transportation.** You can save a bundle by taking public transportation rather than driving to work. It is not a sign of poverty to use public transportation; it's a sign of good sense. If your community doesn't have public transit, join a carpool.

5. **Quit playing the lottery.** Lotteries are nothing more than a tax on the naive. They are a complete waste of money, and the people who spend the most on them can least afford to do so. You might as well throw that money in the fireplace. At least then it will then provide you with some heat.

6. **Eat at cheaper restaurants.** There are marvelous restaurants in your community that serve good food, have good service, and charge a lot less than you're used to paying for a night on the town. To further pinch pennies, save restaurants for special occasions.

7. **Never go grocery shopping on an empty stomach.** This is an inviolable law. You'll buy fewer groceries, and you won't risk serious physical injury from trying to carry five hundred pounds of groceries into your kitchen in a weakened condition.

8. **Stay away from designer labels on everything from clothes to cosmetics.** No wonder clothing designers and cosmetics mavens live in baronial splendor. Have you seen how much they charge for their products? Eschewing these overpriced products may not satisfy your self-image, but it will help your bank account.

9. **Wear wash-and-wear clothing.** You can save a bundle on dry cleaning by wearing wash-and-wear clothing. Whoever invented wrinkle-free clothing should achieve sainthood.

10. **Don't pay extra for extra ingredients.** Paying for soap with moisturizer, for example, or cereal with raisins is almost always considerably more expensive than buying soap and moisturizer or cereal and raisins separately. There are never enough raisins in the cereal with raisins anyway.

11. **Use coupons.** You'll be amazed at how those nickels and dimes add up. A little effort can save you hundreds of dollars per year on groceries. If you shop online, be sure to search for an online coupon offer before making the purchase.

12. **Take vacations closer to home.** There are probably great places to vacation near your hometown. Many people live close to vacation areas that other people travel hundreds or thousands of miles to visit.

A Half-Dozen Ways to Get Quick Cash

Here are six ideas for getting some quick cash, should the need arise.

1. **Work part time.** Moonlighting if you already have a job or working part time if you're between jobs is perhaps the best way for many people to augment their income. Despite the flagging economy, there are still plenty of part-time jobs in many locales. Many employers are

effectively utilizing part-time employees and, in order to attract them, offer flexible working arrangements and working hours.

2. **Tap your home equity.** While obtaining a home equity loan is a lot tougher now, if you already have a home equity line of credit (and your lender hasn't frozen it because of declining home values), you can tap into it for needed cash.

3. **Borrow from your retirement plan at work.** Most workplace retirement plans allow you to borrow up to one-half of your balance up to a maximum of $50,000. While the loan repayments can be stretched out, the loan is due if you leave your job, so this may not be a good way to raise money if you're worried about losing your job.

4. **Withdraw from your Roth IRA.** If you have a Roth IRA, you can withdraw your contributions (but not any earnings on your contributions) without having to pay taxes or penalties.

5. **Tap into your life insurance cash value.** If you have whole life insurance or similar policies that build up cash values, you can borrow up to the full cash value of the policy.

6. **Sell investments.** You can also get your hands on money by selling some investments that you hold in any nonretirement account. If you sell losing investments, and most of us have plenty of those thanks to plummeting stock prices, you won't owe any capital gains taxes, and you can use up to $3,000 of losses per year to offset your other income.

Safe Money Checklist

If Your Expenses Are Increasing
Faster than Your Income

✔ Examine your finances to find ways to close the gap.

✔ Cutting expenses is the best way to reduce the shortfall.

✔ Even if you have to reduce your savings level, save what you can.

✔ Borrowing to pay current expenses should be used only as a last resort.

✔ Prepare a plan that shows how you are going to make ends meet, and stick to it.

7 Getting Your Debts under Control

I think it's time I start reducing my debts, rather than seeing them creep up every month. It's not that there's a problem or anything, although the amounts I pay on the credit card balances seem to be increasing. If this economy gets any worse, the last thing I want to have are a lot of debts to worry about.

Reviewing your loans and getting your debts under control are always good ideas, but in the face of this long economic slowdown, it is doubly important. It's impossible to determine how bad this crisis will become or how long it will last. At a minimum, you don't want your debts to get out of control. Ideally, you can work to reduce them so that you will be better prepared for any burdens this recession may dish out to you. The following will help you evaluate your current debt situation and plan to take better control of your indebtedness.

FIND OUT WHAT YOU OWE

The worksheet that follows will help you summarize your current loans. Don't forget to include all of them. People have a tendency to omit some of their obligations—especially their credit card debt.

Summary of Loans

	Amount Owed	Monthly Payment
Mortgage	$_____	$_____
Home equity loan or second mortgage	_____	_____
Car loan	_____	_____
Credit card and charge account loans	_____	_____
Student loans	_____	_____
Other loans	_____	_____
Totals	$_____	$_____

DETERMINE WHERE YOU STAND

Once you have summarized your loans, you may want to figure out where you stand in relation to various guidelines that indicate whether you have or are approaching a debt level that is too high. Two such guidelines follow.

1. Exclusive of your home mortgage or rent, the total amount of your installment debt should be not more than 20 percent of your yearly after-tax income, and not more than one-third of your discretionary income for one year—in other words, the amount you have left over after housing, food, clothing, and taxes.
2. Another sign that you may be approaching a debt level that is too high is if you are unable to save regularly or you find that the amount you are able to save on a regular basis is decreasing.

Avoid Adding to Your Debt

Once you find out how much you owe, you need to do two things. First, promise yourself that you will not increase any of your current loan balances. Second, keep your promise. This is a two-step process because it's easy to make these kinds of commitments to yourself, but it's a lot harder to keep them—particularly when you look around at all the conspicuous consumption, mostly by people who can ill afford their profligacy.

It's easy to get into the debt trap when, over the past several years, you've been able to rely on a steadily rising income to meet your steadily rising loan payments. However, many people are about to enter a period where they won't be able to rely on raises every year to meet rising living expenses. If so, something has to give, and all too often it means falling behind on loan payments or worse. So don't complicate matters any more than they are now by adding to your debt.

DELEVERAGE, IF YOU CAN

Deleveraging is the unpleasant task of reducing debt. This is what the big corporate lenders have been doing, and the pain is reflected in their minuscule stock prices. Preparing a plan to reduce your loans now, if you can, will be beneficial even if you don't experience any problems as families struggle to keep their finances intact until the crisis subsides. It's never easy to reduce your debts because, with the exception of a home mortgage, you probably have to pay them off with after-tax dollars. For example, to make a $400 car payment, you will have to earn about $600 in order to have $400 left over after taxes are taken out to make the payment.

Balance the Need to Save with the Desire to Reduce Your Loans

If you have managed to accumulate quite a few annoying loans, chances are that you haven't been too diligent on the savings side of the equation. If so, you have to leave enough room in your loan reduction plan to allow for increasing your savings at the same time. As we head into even tougher economic times, not only will you need to get your debts under better control, but you will also have to build up your savings in case you suffer any financial reversals during the down period. Therefore, you have a formidable but important challenge ahead of you, which may be helped by some reductions in your spending. See Chapter 6 for some tips on curtailing your expenses.

You may have some savings and investments set aside, while at the same time you have let your loans creep up. If so, you must address whether to use your savings to reduce some of the loans. It often makes good financial sense to pay off high-interest-rate loans with savings that are almost certainly not earning anywhere near the high interest rates being paid on the loans. However, in view of the tough times ahead, don't deplete your savings in order to pay off loans. It's better to keep some emergency funds set aside in order to meet any unexpected needs during any future difficult economic times.

You really have two choices if you find that your loans are beginning to approach an uncomfortable level. You can wait for hardship to strike, when it will be doubly difficult to get out from under your indebtedness, or you can start now. I think you know which course is preferable. More information on managing your credit is provided in Chapter 19.

Safe Money Checklist

To Get Your Debts under Control

✔ Find out what you owe by preparing a summary of all your current loans.

✔ Avoid adding to your debt. There is no sense trying to reduce loans with one hand if you are adding to them with the other hand.

✔ Prepare a plan to reduce your debt to a more comfortable level.

✔ Don't devote all your spare resources to reducing debt. It is also necessary to build and maintain a sufficient cash reserve to provide for the unexpected.

8 FOREWARNED IS FOREARMED— PREPARING FOR THE UNEXPECTED

This recession is really taking a toll on our finances. We are having so much trouble making ends meet, and we just got two whopping bills for life insurance and house insurance. I think we will let these policies slide so that we can have some breathing room.

Suffering uninsured losses is bad enough during good times, but during tough economic times, it is even worse. Unfortunately, when people find that their finances are pinched, they are tempted to drop some of their insurance coverage. They know they are taking a chance, but tough times call for tough actions. Insurance, however, should be the last thing you drop. Adequate insurance coverage is essential to ensure your long-term financial well-being: a single gap in your insurance coverage could jeopardize a lifetime's worth of sacrifice and savings. If you are confronted with having to make tough choices in your financial life, don't let insurance be a victim. You might think that if you don't have much in the way of assets, you really don't have much to lose by being uninsured. This is not true. Many people who incur medical bills, are sued, or suffer other losses and are not insured, end up having to pay out of their future job earnings.

This chapter will summarize the essential areas of insurance coverage. If you are pinched financially, I will show you ways to reduce your insurance premiums to a more affordable level while maintaining the coverage that you need.

Another concern that many have is what would happen if their insurance company or any other financial institution with which they do business were to go out of business. Some guidance appears at the end of this chapter.

Essential Insurance Coverage

- **Health insurance.** This protects you from the out-of-pocket costs of health care and from large cash outflows during a major illness.
- **Homeowner's insurance.** This insures against property losses, including a home, other structures, personal property, and general contents of the dwelling.
- **Renter's insurance.** This protects the personal possessions of a tenant against theft or destruction.
- **Automobile insurance.** This protects you from large cash outflows for damages resulting from an automobile accident or theft.
- **Extended personal liability (umbrella) insurance.** This protects you from having your personal assets or future earnings forfeited as a result of a personal liability suit. It provides additional protection on top of homeowner's/renter's and automobile liability coverage.
- **Disability insurance.** This replaces part or most of your wage income if you are disabled.
- **Life insurance.** This replaces part or most of your wage income in the event of your death and covers future expenses of your dependents during a readjustment period after your death.

TIPS ON REDUCING YOUR INSURANCE COSTS

Most people pay more than they have to for insurance coverage. There are two ways to reduce your insurance costs. First, you or your agent should shop around for the best premium prices. The insurance industry is very price-competitive these days, and people have told me numerous times that by taking a little initiative, or prodding their agents to take some initiative, they have been able to save hundreds of dollars on their annual insurance costs. Second, make sure you pay only for the policy features and options you need. All too often, people purchase a "Rolls-Royce" policy when a "Ford" would suit them just fine.

The following suggestions will help you save some insurance money at a time when you could probably use the money for other worthwhile purposes. One of the few good things to come out of bad economic times is that we are forced—out of fear, if not financial necessity—to become wiser consumers. I hope that you will carry these good habits, including being a wiser insurance consumer, forward when prosperity returns anew.

Health Insurance

If you are fortunate enough to have your health insurance provided or, more likely, subsidized by your employer, be sure you understand what it does and doesn't provide.

- You may be offered a choice of plans, each of which offers different types of coverage. Thinking that they shouldn't skimp on health insurance, many people automatically select the policy that costs the most. Instead, you should select the policy that provides the kind of coverage that you and your family need—and it may not be the most expensive policy.

- If you have to buy health insurance on your own, it is almost always cheaper to do so as a member of a group rather than as an individual. You may be able to obtain this coverage through a professional organization or some other local group, such as the Chamber of Commerce, that offers group health insurance to its members. Your state may also be able to steer you to lower-cost coverage.

Homeowner's/Renter's Insurance

There are a few ways that you can reduce your homeowner's or renter's insurance premium without affecting the coverage that you need.

- Obtain quotes from a number of insurance companies. Many homeowners and renters have been delighted to learn how much they can save by changing from their current insurer to another insurer.
- Whatever company you choose, ask how you can reduce your premium. For example, taking measures to improve home security may result in a premium reduction, although, of course, you will have to incur the up-front cost in order to receive the premium reduction.
- Most people select a low deductible on their homeowner's or renter's insurance without thinking. If you have a bit of a financial cushion—in other words, if you can afford to pay, say, the first $1,000 of a loss—select a higher deductible and save some premium dollars.

Automobile Insurance

Ways to reduce your auto insurance premiums abound.

- Increasing the deductible on your collision coverage to $500 from $200 could reduce your collision insurance cost by 15 to 30 percent. You may want to consider dropping your collision coverage or comprehensive coverage if you drive an old car, as I do.
- You may be able to eliminate some of the medical coverage on your auto policy if it duplicates coverage that you already have on your health-insurance policy.
- The total cost of insurance is affected by the type of car you drive. Buying a "low-profile" car, one that's less costly to repair and less attractive to thieves, will save you premium dollars. It will also save you money when you buy the car in the first place, since these cars are as unattractive to car devotees as they are to thieves, but who cares (other than your kids, who, by the way, aren't paying for the car)?

Disability Insurance

Disability income insurance provided by your employer may or may not be sufficient to meet your needs in terms of policy provisions and extent of coverage. If you have to purchase this absolutely essential coverage individually, the following suggestions may save you some money. Incidentally, you have to have a job in order to have a disability policy.

- As with health insurance, many professional organizations and affinity groups provide disability insurance coverage for their members, which is much cheaper than individually purchased policies.

- If you do purchase an individual policy, you'll be dismayed at how expensive it is. Disability policies have more options than most new cars. Some may be worthwhile, such as cost-of-living adjustments for benefits, but don't buy any bells and whistles that you don't need.

Life Insurance

When economic times get tough, many people see dropping some or all of their life insurance coverage as an easy way to cut expenses. Instead of reducing your coverage and jeopardizing your family's security, try to make the most of your life insurance dollar by heeding the following suggestions.

- You may have too much life insurance. If so, you can save money by dropping unnecessary coverage. Life insurance needs change and in some instances decline, particularly after children leave the nest. Review your coverage periodically to ensure that you have an appropriate amount.
- There are plenty of ways to buy low-cost life insurance coverage if you devote some time to it. It will be time well spent, because identical life insurance policies vary dramatically in price. Why pay more for something as dull as life insurance? First, your employer may offer you the option of buying additional coverage, usually at low group rates. Next, comparison-shop for life insurance coverage on the Internet or by simply asking friends and colleagues if they are aware of companies that offer low-cost life insurance. If you decide to replace a more expensive policy with a cheaper policy, always obtain the new coverage before dropping the old policy.

- Avoid credit life insurance that may be sold to you when you take out a loan. Credit life insurance will pay off your loan if you die while the loan is outstanding. This insurance is almost always horrendously expensive.

WHAT HAPPENS IF YOUR BANK, MORTGAGE LENDER, BROKER, OR INSURANCE COMPANY GOES OUT OF BUSINESS?

There have been a lot of financial institution failures lately, but fortunately, you generally are protected. However, your protection varies based on the type and size of account you have.

Bank Failure

Some of your best protection comes if you invest with a bank or savings institution that is insured by the Federal Deposit Insurance Corporation (FDIC) or a credit union that is insured by the National Credit Union Share Insurance Fund (NCUSIF). Generally, the FDIC or NCUSIF, backed by the U.S. government, covers each person to $100,000 per institution. However, because of the financial meltdown of 2008, Congress extended that amount to $250,000 through the end of 2009. Beware of putting $250,000 in a long-term CD that matures in 2010 or later, though. The higher limit may not be extended to cover your entire term.

There are ways to get federal insurance for much more money at a single institution than these limits. That's because you may get separate FDIC or NCUSIF insurance protection for different categories of account ownership. Right now, for example, a family can get $250,000 worth of coverage through 2009 (or later if Congress extends the temporary regulations) in each of the following categories:

- Single accounts, titled in one person's name.
- Retirement accounts, such as IRAs and SIMPLE plans.
- Joint bank accounts owned by two or more people. They are insured to $250,000 per joint owner.
- Revocable trust accounts, also known as "payable on death" accounts.

Trust accounts are covered to $250,000 per account holder and another $250,000 per beneficiary.

Make sure you don't exceed those insurance limits, however, by going to www.myfdicinsurance.gov or calling 1-877-ASK-FDIC. Federal laws severely restrict the FDIC's ability to reimburse depositors who exceed coverage limits.

When an FDIC-insured institution fails, it typically is closed and reopened the next business day, although longer delays may arise for some holders of complex trust accounts and deposits held by brokerage firms.

The federal insurance coverage kicks in at the institution's date of failure, and includes interest. Generally, the FDIC may find another institution to acquire a failed institution; sell the insured deposits, but hold on to uninsured deposits and assets; or run the institution until it can find a buyer.

During a bank failure, checks may inadvertently bounce if they're clearing at the time an institution is closed. But if you're charged any fees, the FDIC suggests that you ask to be reimbursed, and it encourages FDIC-insured institutions to provide reimbursement.

Have a certificate of deposit at a failed bank? If another institution acquires your deposits, you may be given the option of accepting a lower interest rate or withdrawing your funds without penalty.

Lender Failure

Sad to report, but if your lender goes bankrupt, you still must continue to make mortgage and loan payments to the bankrupt lender as scheduled until you are notified by a new owner of the loan. If a mortgage company fails and you're in the middle of a mortgage problem, contact your state mortgage regulator for assistance.

Brokerage or Mutual Fund Firm Failure

Unlike with bank or credit union accounts, you assume most of the risk if you own stocks, bonds, mutual funds, or exchange-traded funds. That's why you need to do your homework carefully, stick with good-quality investments, and make sure you're well diversified.

Expect no financial backing from the U.S. government if the value of those investments drops. Despite numerous government bailouts, you and I aren't going to be bailed out from our losing investments. In virtually all cases, when a brokerage firm fails, customer assets are safely transferred to another registered brokerage firm. The same applies to mutual fund companies. The Securities Investor Protection Corp. (SIPC) also covers you up to $500,000, including $100,000 in cash, if your brokerage firm or mutual fund company is a member. But that coverage does not cover market losses. Nor does it cover investments in commodity futures, fixed annuities, currency, hedge funds, or investment contracts, like limited partnerships that are not SEC-registered. About the only circumstance in which SIPC might step in is in the highly unlikely possibility that your assets are missing at a brokerage house. Many brokerage firms and mutual fund companies provide substantial additional private insurance coverage on top of SIPC coverage.

Once liquidation starts, most brokerage customers can expect to get their assets in one to three months, according to the Financial Industry Regulatory Authority (FINRA).

Insurance Company Failure

If your insurance company fails, your state insurance commissioner will take control of the company's operations or appoint a receiver. Each state has an insurance guaranty association to protect policyholders of licensed insurance companies. The guaranty association, the insurance commissioner, and the receiver determine whether the company can be rehabilitated or whether it should be liquidated. If it is liquidated, policies are generally transferred to a financially sound insurance company.

Therefore, you should be okay on your life, health, and property and casualty insurance. State insurance guaranties are limited, but you should generally have in the range of $100,000 to $300,000 worth of coverage.

With respect to annuities, coverage on a fixed-rate annuity is similar to coverage on other insurance areas outlined previously. Money invested in a variable-rate annuity is, by law, separated from the insurance company's accounts, so it is insulated from a bankruptcy of the insurer that issued your policy; but the investments in the variable annuity are not protected from market declines.

PROTECTING AGAINST THE FAILURE OF A FINANCIAL INSTITUTION

In order to minimize any problems—or, more likely, inconveniences—from a financial institution failure, always keep good records of your accounts. Here are some additional tips.

Insurance Companies

- Stick with only the financially strongest insurance companies, rated A+ and A++ by A.M. Best and AAA by Standard & Poor's. The protection that state guaranty associations provide may not be sufficient.
- If you need a particularly large life insurance policy, split it among different insurers.
- Contact your state insurance commissioner if you experience problems during a failure. Go to www.naic.org for contact information.

Banks, Savings Institutions, and Credit Unions

- Make sure that your deposit is in a federally insured bank or credit union account. Not all institutions are insured.
- Remember that annuities, bonds, and mutual funds that you may hold at the bank are not covered by federal insurance.
- If you purchase a CD from a broker, make sure the records show that the broker is merely acting as an agent for you and the other owners. They might read, for example, "XYZ Brokerage as Custodian for Customers." Otherwise you may not get FDIC coverage. Also, be sure that your broker doesn't place your money in institutions in which you may already have funds, putting you over the FDIC limits.
- Make certain that you stay within federal insurance limits at each FDIC-insured institution. Some institutions— despite different names—may be under the same charter. If they are under one charter, the FDIC would consider them to be the same bank.

- Keep less than the FDIC maximum in a CD or other interest-bearing account. Otherwise interest could put you over coverage limits.
- Get instructions on what to do if your bank fails at www.fdic.gov.

Brokerage and Mutual Fund Firms

- Check the brokerage firm with your state securities regulator, which you can find at www.nasaa.org, for complaints before you invest.
- Make certain that your brokerage and/or mutual fund firm is covered by the SIPC. Ideally, the firm should also provide additional private insurance coverage.
- Stick with large, reputable brokerages and mutual fund companies.
- Carefully check all your broker's periodic statements. If you disagree with anything, write a letter stating that you don't agree with the accuracy of the statement. Without a written record of dispute, there may be no reason for anybody to believe you if you file a claim saying that valuable securities are missing from your account.
- In the event of a failure, gather brokerage account records, statements, and trade confirmations.
- Go to the SIPC Web site at www.sipc.org for contact information if you hear of a liquidation that involves your firm. Follow SIPC instructions in filling out the necessary forms, and pay strict attention to time limits in the notice and claim form.

Safe Money Checklist

Preparing for the Unexpected

Be sure you have adequate coverage in each of the following areas:

✔ Health insurance
   ✔ Homeowner's or renter's insurance
   ✔ Automobile insurance
   ✔ Extended personal liability (umbrella) insurance
   ✔ Disability insurance
   ✔ Life insurance

✔ Continuing your insurance coverage must be a high-priority item in your budget. If you are experiencing financial stress, don't be tempted to let this vital coverage lapse.

✔ Look for ways to reduce your insurance costs in each area of coverage. With a moderate amount of effort, you may be able to save hundreds of dollars.

✔ Do business only with highly rated insurance and financial companies to avoid the inconvenience of having an account with a company that goes bankrupt.

✔ Understand your protections if one of the insurance or financial companies with which you do business goes bankrupt.

Part III

Investing in Tough Economic Times

9 INVESTMENT STRATEGIES FOR FRIGHTENED INVESTORS

When the stock market took a big dive, I had no idea what to do, and the financial commentators were no help. Some of them said get out of stocks, while others said it was a great buying opportunity. But I did nothing, and stocks sank yet again. I've lost a lot of money, and I can't afford any more mistakes.

The next few years will not be easy ones for investors. No matter how much or how little you have to invest, you probably have recently been tempted to sell all your investments and put your money in the safest possible securities. If you are frightened and preoccupied about losing money on your investments, it could make sense, for your own peace of mind, for you to "go into cash," as Wall Street says (see Chapter 14). But there is a danger in taking this course, just as there is a danger in putting all your money into stocks. The problem with being overly conservative is that, over the long run, your investments won't grow nearly as much as they would if you had some other, admittedly riskier, securities in your investment portfolio. On the other hand, the danger of putting all your eggs in the "stock basket" is that stocks do periodically decline in value, sometimes significantly, as the recent stock crash painfully illustrates. Investors who had all or most of their money in stocks during the crash are obviously a lot poorer, on paper at least, than they would have been had they spread their money over other kinds of investments.

In this chapter, you will learn ways to structure your investments so that you can invest wisely without losing sleep. Depending on your outlook, I will show you several ways to invest. You may be optimistic about the prospects for stocks and bonds going forward. If you are pessimistic, you have every reason to be. But most likely you, like most people, have no idea what is going to happen. You want to invest so that you can take advantage of a market rebound when it occurs, yet you want some protection against market adversity as well.

Before I get into specific investment strategies, I'll explain in this chapter about *investment allocation*, which means deciding how much of your money you will invest in each of the various investment categories. Investment allocation is not difficult to understand, and it is crucially important to your long-term investment success.

This is the first of six investment chapters, giving you a foundation to help you better understand the information that follows. Chapter 10 presents ten rules for investing successfully during tough times. Tips for making the right stock, bond, real estate, and temporary investments during this rough economic climate are offered in Chapters 11 through 14. One final note: these chapters don't assume that you have $10 million to invest. The information provided should help you even if you're just starting out or restarting to build your investments. I will frequently use the word *portfolio* to describe all of your investment holdings. You may think that the word applies only to those who have enormous sums of money. That's not the case, though. Even if you have all of your money in a single stock mutual fund, you have a portfolio of stocks, and you are encouraged to impress your acquaintances in describing your portfolio.

INVESTMENT CATEGORIES

Saving regularly and investing those savings wisely are the two most important things you can do to meet major financial obligations during your lifetime, cope with financial emergencies that may occur as a result of the economic crisis or other future adversity, and ultimately achieve financial security. As you will find in this and the following investment chapters, it's not that difficult to be a good investor, one who can make sensible investment decisions on her own or by working with an experienced and competent investment advisor. There are four major categories of investments.

1. **Stocks** can be purchased by buying individual shares directly or by buying stock mutual funds. The haughty refer to stocks as *equities*. (See Chapter 11.)
2. **Bonds** can be purchased directly or through bond mutual funds. A bond pays interest until it matures, and the principal is then returned to the investor. While the interest rate on a bond stays the same (that's why bonds are often called *fixed-income investments*), its value can fluctuate depending upon changes in interest rates. (See Chapter 12.)

3. **Real estate** investments can be most easily acquired by buying real estate stocks or a real estate mutual fund. Some investors prefer to buy individual properties. The following discussion on investment allocation will consider primarily interest-earning investments and stocks, since most people choose not to invest in properties (except for their own home). (See Chapter 13.)

4. **Safe investments** are securities that pay interest with no risk of losing principal and that can be sold very easily. The price that is paid for safety and liquidity is that the investment returns on safe investments are usually lower than could be obtained with the other investment categories. (See Chapter 14.)

INVESTMENT ALLOCATION

Investment allocation (also called investment diversification) means deciding how much of your investment portfolio, however large or small it might be, should be invested in stocks and how much should be in bonds and temporary (safe) investments. For the sake of illustration, bonds and temporary investments will be combined into a single category called "interest-earning investments," since investors earn interest on both of these types. All too often, investors tend to invest in extremes, placing too much emphasis on one category or the other. Even though they may think they are investing wisely, they are probably not doing so if they have most of their money in stocks or most of it in interest-earning securities. Do you know how your investments are allocated right now? Most people don't have any idea. But you should, so space to fill in your current allocation is provided in the table below. This is optional, but Professor Pond will give you a better grade if you dig up the numbers. By the way, you should combine all of your investment accounts to get a good view of how your money is divided up. It can be misleading to break down one or two accounts when you have others that are not included.

My Current Investment Allocation	
Stocks and stock funds*	_____ %
Interest-earning securities	_____ %
Total	100%

* If you own real estate stocks or real estate mutual funds, include them on the "stocks and stock funds" line.

Why concern yourself with how your investments are allocated? First, investors tend to focus too much on the short term under any circumstances, and even more so when the investment markets are awful. In 2008, the investment markets were decidedly so, with stocks tanking, most bonds declining in value, and the interest paid on temporary investments being about enough to pay for a burger and small fries. No matter how bad the short-term outlook may be, however, the long-term outlook is better. Therefore, for money that you're going to need for the long term, say a decade or longer (which is probably most of your money), a sensibly allocated portfolio will produce the best return with a reasonable level of risk.

Second, a common response to scary investment markets is to put most or all of your money into safe investments. Although this may be the best place to be if the stock market keeps dropping forever, an illustration in Chapter 11 reveals that stock market rebounds usually begin before there's a clear indication that the economy is on the mend. Missing these often fast rebounds will almost certainly drag down long-term performance. This is not to say that investors should necessarily be going into stocks in a big way, either. What's important is striking a balance between stocks and interest-earning securities.

The 60/40 Solution

The task at hand, and I can't overstate how important it is, is how to divide up your long-term investment money, that is, money you're not going to need to spend within a few years, between stocks and interest-earning securities. The "60/40 solution" is the basis upon which you and I can figure out how you should be allocating your money. By this I mean investing 60 percent of your long-term investment money in stocks and 40 percent in interest-earning securities. Most of the studies on the subject of investment allocation have suggested that an investment mix of 60 percent stocks and 40 percent interest-earning securities is an excellent way for most investors to balance the two investment objectives of earning an inflation-beating return while not taking too much risk. If your investment diversification varies considerably from these parameters, you may be taking too much or too little risk. We'll soon find out.

A 60 percent stock/40 percent interest-earning investment allocation is not cast in concrete. Rather, consider it a benchmark around which you customize your own diversification strategy. One major ingredient in coming up with a diversification model that fits you is how comfortable you are with investment risk.

What Kind of Investor Are You?

If you're going to join the "sleep at night" investor club, you have to decide how comfortable you are with the inevitable fluctuations in stock and bond prices. Investors fall into one of three general categories depending on how well they can tolerate periodic dips in the value of their investments:

- An **aggressive investor** wants to achieve high long-term investment returns, even if that means that the investments will periodically experience heart-stopping short-term declines in value.
- A **moderate investor** wants to achieve a balance between earning attractive long-term investment returns and moderating periodic fluctuations in value.
- A **conservative investor** seeks stable growth in his investments, even if that means somewhat lower returns over time. A conservative investor is not as comfortable as other investors with the ups and downs of the stock market. If you're inclined to prefer this classification because your investment portfolio is now a mere wisp of what it once was thanks to the credit crisis, bear in mind that this may not be the way you would like to invest over the next several years once the stock market gets back to normal, whenever that might be.

Investment Diversification Illustrations

Depending on whether you're an aggressive, moderate, or conservative investor, here are examples of ways to allocate your investments. The essence of successful investing is to divvy up your money along the lines suggested here. Periodically rebalancing your investments, which is explained in Chapter 10, is icing on the cake. All this may sound complicated and time-consuming, but it isn't. One other note before delving into the numbers: whenever you see the terms *stocks* and *interest-earning*, I mean either individual stocks and interest-earning securities or stock mutual funds and interest-earning securities mutual funds, like bond funds and money market funds.

If You're an Aggressive Investor

Stocks	70–90%
Interest-earning	10–30%
Total	100%

If You're a Moderate Investor

Stocks	40–70%
Interest-earning	30–60%
Total	100%

If You're a Conservative Investor

Stocks	20–40%
Interest-earning	60–80%
Total	100%

Try to Be Consistent, Even during Periods of Maximum Pessimism

If you have the wisdom to devise and then stick with a sensible approach to investing, the biggest investment challenge you'll have to confront from here on out is to avoid the temptation to abandon your plan. The stock market has and will periodically scare the bejeepers out of you. All worthwhile long-term investments will occasionally lose value, and in the past it has sometimes taken years to recoup the losses. But patience is a virtue that should help you make up for lost ground—and then some.

Tweaking Your Investment Allocation

The investment allocation summaries that are based on your risk comfort level provide ranges rather than fixed percentages. This gives you some wiggle room to tweak your allocation when you think investment conditions merit a bit of a change in your investments. After all, you need some peace of mind. For example, take the case of a moderate investor who was maintaining a 60 percent stock and 40 percent interest-earning allocation. The market is shaky, and the investor is getting uncomfortable. So she decides to move her allocation from 60 percent stock down to 50 percent stock, a move that will not radically change her allocation but will still make her more comfortable. This tweaking can work the other way as well. An optimistic investor who believes that stock prices are at bargain levels could increase his stock exposure without risking going overboard on stocks.

What's Your Preference?

The primary advantage of investment allocation, and it is a huge advantage, is that it moderates the effects of big moves in the stock market. Should the weak economy continue to weigh on the stock market, the presence of interest-earning securities can reduce the impact of any further deterioration in stock prices on your overall portfolio returns. Including both categories of investments means that you'll almost always have some money invested in a category that's thriving without having too much money in a category that's diving. Here's a revealing statistic: over the past 75 years, both stocks *and* bonds lost value in the same year only three times. The table below shows how important investment allocation can be. It assumes that the interest-earning portion of the portfolio earns 5 percent per year. Thus, an investor who has a 60 percent stock/40 percent interest-earning allocation during a year in which stocks take a 30 percent drubbing would have a 16 percent portfolio loss, about half the overall stock loss. Check this table against your desired allocation percentages to see how your investments would fare in both rising and declining stock markets. Chances are you'll be pleasantly surprised.

What's Your Investment Allocation Preference?

Investment Allocation	100% stocks	80% stocks	60% stocks	40% stocks	20% stocks	0% stocks
Change in portfolio if stock market						
Rises						
+10%	+10%	+8%	+8%	+7%	+6%	+5%
+20%	+20%	+16%	+14%	+11%	+8%	+5%
+30%	+30%	+24%	+20%	+15%	+10%	+5%
+40%	+40%	+32%	+26%	+19%	+12%	+5%
+50%	+50%	+40%	+32%	+23%	+14%	+5%
Falls						
−10%	−10%	−7%	−4%	−1%	+2%	+5%
−20%	−20%	−15%	−10%	−5%	0%	+5%
−30%	−30%	−23%	−16%	−9%	−2%	+5%
−40%	−40%	−31%	−22%	−13%	−4%	+5%
−50%	−50%	−39%	−28%	−17%	−6%	+5%

Safe Money Checklist

Investment Strategies for Frightened Investors

✔ Become familiar with the various investment categories and the role each should play in putting together a diversified portfolio.

✔ Combine all of your investment accounts to find out how your money is currently divvied up between stocks and interest-earning securities.

✔ Give some thought to whether you are an aggressive, moderate, or conservative investor.

✔ Based on your investment preference, decide roughly how you would like to divide your investments between stocks and interest-earning securities.

10 TEN RULES FOR INVESTING SUCCESSFULLY IN TURBULENT MARKETS

My investments are a mess, I think. Even though I don't have much in the way of investments, the money is important to me, and sometimes I feel that I should be making some of the moves that the experts suggest. Other times I get so worried that I think about selling everything

*and putting my money in a savings account. It's tough
enough investing when times are good, but who knows
what to do when the economy is in turmoil—with no
end in sight?*

Several long-standing investing rules of thumb have been
sternly refuted as a result of the turmoil in the investment
markets, and none more than the assertion that if you hold onto
stocks for at least 10 years, you can't lose. The 2008 stock market dive has probably wiped out more than a decade of gains.
This chapter contains 10 straightforward rules for successful
investing in both abysmal and ebullient markets. They will help
you invest sensibly in a rough and unpredictable economy,
whether you have $1,000 or $1,000,000 to invest, without rely-
ing on tenuous rules of thumb.

These 10 rules are probably not going to make you rich in the
next couple of years, but they won't make you poor either. Many
of them can help you invest successfully in any market, but they
are *essential* in tough markets. People who get themselves into
trouble with their investments during unpredictable and volatile
markets inevitably violate at least one of these rules. Yet, the rules
aren't that difficult or time-consuming to follow.

1. THE GOLDEN RULE OF INVESTING

The Golden Rule of Investing is: thou canst not predict the market.

The investment allocation guidelines described in Chapter 9
and the rebalancing suggestions presented in Rule 5 in this chapter are intended to take the guesswork out of investing in both

stocks and interest-earning securities. Nevertheless, you'll still be tempted to try to predict future investment performance and act on your prediction—that's called market timing. After all, just about everyone else tries it. The allure of market timing is certainly understandable. Long bull markets make investors skittish. Quick market downturns scare everyone. The notion that you can actually get out of the market just before it takes a dip and then get back into the market just before it rebounds is terribly attractive.

Market Timing Doesn't Work

The big challenge in trying to time the stock market is not so much getting out of the market before it drops or before it drops further as it is deciding when to get back in, which is exactly the predicament confronting the legions of investors who recently fled the stock market. This reminds me of a caller on a radio talk show who told me that he had taken his money out of stocks entirely quite a while ago, and he was wondering if it was a good time to get back in. It turns out this poor chap had been trying to figure out the best time to get back into stocks for many years. In the meantime, the stock market had quadrupled.

Once you recognize that you'll never be able to predict the near-term performance of the investment markets, you can confidently devise a diversified investment strategy and stick with it, even when you're losing money and the Wall Street pundits are spewing out nothing but awful forecasts.

2. TAKE A LONG-TERM VIEW

We are all too familiar with the havoc recessions can wreak on our money. Stock and real estate prices have declined. Interest rates on some securities have declined, in some instances to record low levels. Rates on other securities have risen, depressing bond prices. That's a recipe for both angst and, if you react to such concerns, mediocre investment performance. No wonder so many investors are focusing on the short term. Rather than worrying about where your stocks and interest-earning securities will be 10 minutes, or 10 days, or even 10 months from now, focus on how they are likely to fare 10 and 20 years from now. What possible good can come from obsessing over what happened to your stocks yesterday or what will happen to them next week? Take a long-term view instead, because most of the money you have probably won't be needed for a long time. Your health and your wealth will both benefit.

3. KEEP ADDING TO YOUR INVESTMENTS

Whether you already have a sizable portfolio, are a beginner, or are somewhere in between, the best way to build up your investments is by regularly adding to your investments and regularly increasing the amount of new money you add. One of the easiest ways to increase your investments is to reinvest your dividends, capital gains, and interest rather than leave them in a low-yield money market fund.

Dollar Cost Averaging

But you can supercharge your investments even more by investing new money at regular intervals. This is precisely what is being done by everyone who participates in a retirement savings plan at work [401(k), 403(b), and other such plans]. Dollar cost averaging is the process of investing a fixed amount on a regular basis. The trick is to stick with your schedule, regardless of whether stock or bond prices go up or down. Because you're investing a fixed amount at fixed intervals, your dollars buy fewer shares when stock, stock fund, or bond fund prices are high and more when they are low. As a result, the average purchase price is lower than the average market price over the same time frame. In plain English, you're buying more when prices are low. You can't beat that.

4. Don't Let Your Age Dictate the Way You Invest

Most people think that their age has a big bearing on how they should invest. In short, younger people think they can afford a lot of risk, so they put all or most of their money into stocks or real estate. Older people, particularly retirees, may think that it's time to be very conservative in their investments, and the recent stock market rout reinforces that opinion. In some respects age is relevant, but not as much as many people believe, particularly those who think they're too old to afford big investment losses. The primary way in which age determines how you should invest is how long you'll need to rely on your nest egg to support you, your so-called investment horizon. Since it's prudent to plan on a life expectancy of at least age 95, even people who have recently retired will need their money to last for at least two decades. The oldest members of the baby boom generation have an investment horizon of around 30 years, while the youngest boomers have an investment horizon of about 50 years. In considering how you should diversify your investments, there isn't a lot of difference between 30 years and 50 years.

During the 2008 bear market, a lot of attention was focused on the plight of the many preretirees and retirees who lost a large percentage of their life's savings. The common lament was that they were sunk financially because they didn't have enough time to make up for their investment losses. Many felt that they couldn't afford to lose any more money, so they moved what they had left into safe investments. Who could blame them? At a time when stocks were losing over 10 percent a month, making 2 percent on government money market funds looked awfully good. But most preretirees and recent retirees still need to keep at least some of their money in stocks so that they can provide the growth necessary to pay ever-increasing living expenses during a long retirement. Avoid the trap of pulling out of stocks after you have lost a lot of money, only to miss the rebound in the stock market. You're probably not "too old" for stocks, since you have plenty of time to make up for your losses.

5. REBALANCE YOUR INVESTMENTS PERIODICALLY

If you have paid close attention to how you allocate (diversify) your investments (as described in Chapter 9) and you have selected good investments (see Chapters 11 to 14), it's hard not to be a successful investor. But periodically rebalancing your investments is an additional step that should further improve the returns on your investments.

Here's how rebalancing works. You first need to establish a diversification target for your investments, as illustrated in Chapter 9—for example, 60 percent in stocks and 40 percent in interest-earning investments. Over time, the investments you own will change in value. After one year, let's assume your allocation has changed from 60 percent stocks and 40 percent interest-earning to 55 percent stocks and 45 percent interest-earning because the stock market has declined. The task at hand is to rebalance by buying enough stocks and selling a like amount of bonds to get back to the 60 percent/40 percent target allocation. Why is rebalancing a good thing? Because rebalancing forces you to buy stocks on the cheap—after they've fallen in value—at a time when the Wall Street herd is abandoning them. Rebalancing also forces you to sell stocks after they've risen in value, which you would have done during the bull market of 2003–2007. Those who just let their money ride during that time without rebalancing probably entered 2008 with far too much of their money in stocks, which hammered their portfolios a lot more than would have been the case had they gradually reduced their stock holdings by rebalancing. The other thing that rebalancing does is to force you to buy bonds after interest rates have risen, which is exactly what you want to do—lock in higher bond interest rates. Since rebalancing usually involves only small shifts in your overall investment holdings, you're not making a major move, which is a good thing under any market conditions.

6. BUY OR SELL GRADUALLY

Investors who make major changes in their investments quickly almost always end up worse off than they would be if they had made them gradually. Rebalancing usually involves small moves, but there also may be times when you simply want to make some changes on your own, or when you have money sitting on the sidelines that you want to invest. If so, do so gradually. For example, perhaps you are really concerned about the recent performance of a stock or mutual fund that you own. There's no law that says you have to sell the entire holding. You might plan to sell half now and wait on selling the other half. Another example: say interest rates rise to the point where you find bonds to be particularly attractive, and you would like to invest. Again, don't commit all of the money you would like to add to bonds at once. After all, interest rates could rise even further, and you don't want a lot of your money stuck in bonds if interest rates continue to rise.

7. Avoid Traps in Workplace Retirement Savings Plans

While most employees don't realize it, most 401(k) and 403(b) plans offer primarily stock mutual fund choices. It's not unusual for 80 percent or more of the choices to be stock funds. Many plan participants who spread their money among a variety of funds in the plan may think they're well diversified, but they end up with far too much money invested in stocks. As a result, employees report that they have lost as much as half or more of their workplace retirement plan money because of the stock market meltdown. To avoid this trap, pay more attention to how your money is allocated between stock and interest-earning fund choices rather than simply putting money blindly into a bunch of stock funds that could result in further big losses if the stock market continues to stumble.

Putting some money in terrible fund choices is another trap. Unfortunately, many 401(k) and 403(b) plans are filled with fund choices that are nothing short of pitiful. The only excuse for investing in them is if a close relative is managing the fund. Be sure your selections are up to snuff, and avoid any that are not.

8. USE ALL-IN-ONE FUNDS TO IMPROVE INVESTMENT RETURNS

All-in-one investments are the perfect antidote for investors who are concerned that they're going to make mistakes in their investing, especially when the investment markets are so troubling. All-in-one investments allow you to invest money—even a small amount—in a single fund that diversifies across several important investment categories. These "set it and forget it" investments are ideal for those who simply don't want to be bothered with the chore of selecting and monitoring their investment holdings. They hold mutual funds with solid performance histories or individual stocks and bonds that are actively managed. They also regularly and automatically rebalance your holdings, as was recommended in Rule 5. Many mutual fund families, insurance companies, and brokerage firms have introduced a stable of all-in-one funds. They are often available in workplace retirement plans like 401(k) and 403(b) plans and tax-sheltered annuities. Their main attraction is the simplicity of a single all-purpose fund rather than having to pick from among a long list of retirement savings plan choices. Even if you're into investing actively, all-in-one investments deserve a good look. There are three categories of all-in one funds:

- **Balanced funds** usually maintain a fixed allocation of your money, typically 60 percent in stocks, primarily conservative large-company stocks, and 40 percent in U.S. government and corporate bonds and temporary investments. These aren't as diversified as the other all-in-one fund choices, but they have usually done very well over the years.

- **Lifestyle funds** diversify your money across several investment categories according to how comfortable you are with investment risk. They are usually offered as a series of mutual funds under such names as "income," "conservative," "moderate," and "growth." Each individual fund is managed using a designated allocation of stocks, bonds, and temporary investments. For example, a growth fund would hold a much higher percentage of stocks than a conservative fund, which would be more heavily invested in bonds. One of the beauties of lifestyle funds is that if you want to invest a bit less or a bit more in stocks, you can simply move your money between categories. For example, if you hold a moderate fund but you are becoming concerned about stock losses, you can move to a conservative fund that will hold a lower percentage of stocks compared with the moderate fund.
- **Target date funds** diversify and gradually adjust your diversification according to a fund's target date. While most people select a target date fund based upon the year they expect to retire, they can also move money between target date funds in order to adjust the overall investment allocation. The closer the target date is to the present, the lower the percentage of stocks that are held in the fund. For example, a typical 2015 target date fund would hold about 20 percent less stocks than a 2025 fund.

9. AVERAGE IS PRETTY GOOD—USE EXCHANGE-TRADED FUNDS AND INDEX FUNDS

The majority of actively managed mutual funds underperform their benchmark indexes. For example, most large-company stock funds would underperform a large-company stock index, like the Standard & Poor's 500 Stock Index. During the recent stock market implosion, many mutual funds had a particularly tough time containing their losses. While actively managed mutual funds struggled, exchange-traded funds (ETFs) and index funds did what they are supposed to do: generate average investment returns. ETFs are like mutual funds in that they hold a bunch of individual stocks and/or bonds, but ETFs are bought and sold on the stock exchange, rather than from a mutual fund company. Most ETFs are designed to match the returns of a particular stock index, like the aforementioned S&P 500. An index fund is very similar to an ETF in operation. The primary difference is that you buy an index fund from a mutual fund company rather than on the stock exchange. The costs of owning these funds are very low, and you may be able to reap some tax advantages as well.

The vast majority of investors can't even manage to keep up with the stock index averages, so being able to just be average with ETFs or index funds can put you in the top half of the investor class. It is possible to find mutual funds that outperform the index averages pretty consistently, but you or your investment advisor needs to devote the time necessary to identify and monitor them. What's the solution? As in every other area of your financial life, deciding between ETFs or index funds and actively managed funds is not an "either/or" decision. Why not use a little of both?

10. Consider Annuities for Lifetime Income

Income annuities will be receiving a lot of attention in light of the huge losses so many have suffered in the stock market and the uncertainty about the future of the investment markets. Reports of people nearing or in retirement who lost substantial portions of their nest eggs have given new credence to the relative safety of an income annuity. Income annuities are like a personal pension plan, so they are particularly propitious for the growing number of employees who work for employers that don't provide pension plans.

- **If you're still in the workforce.** Working-age people, particularly those who are within a decade of retirement and who are concerned about protecting some of their retirement money from further losses, might consider moving some money into a deferred annuity that provides a decent rate of interest. Then, at or after retirement, the fixed annuity can be moved into an income annuity that will provide lifetime income.

- **If you're a retiree.** Consider using a portion of your retirement stash to purchase an income annuity so that you'll have the comfort of knowing that the annuity plus social security will provide you with lifetime income no matter how badly the investment markets might fare in the future. You may want to consider purchasing income annuities gradually during your retirement years. For example, you might give one a test run now. If you're happy with that one, you could purchase another a few years hence.

Safe Money Checklist

Rules for Successful Investing

✔ Always keep the Golden Rule of Investing in mind. No one can predict how the investment markets will fare, particularly in the near future.

✔ Avoid obsessing over how the markets will fare over the short term. Always take a long-term view.

✔ Your age is less a factor in determining how you should invest than how long you're going to need your money to last.

✔ Keep adding to your investments by saving regularly and reinvesting your interest, dividends, and capital gains. Let the miracle of saving and compounding make you financially secure no matter how the investment markets are performing.

✔ Rebalancing your investments periodically will help you moderate the risk of simply letting your investments ride and help you make well-timed decisions to add to or reduce certain holdings.

✔ Buy or sell your investments gradually. Avoid making sudden changes in your investments, even in the current unsettling investment environment.

✔ Avoid unwittingly putting too much of your workplace retirement savings plan money into stocks. Also avoid putting money into any mediocre fund choices in your plan at work.

✔ All-in-one funds can ease the chore of riding herd on your investments while ensuring that you maintain a well-diversified portfolio.

✔ Consider using exchange-traded funds and index funds. While they produce only average investment returns, average is pretty good for most investors.

✔ If you are retired or approaching retirement, annuities can provide an immediate or future source of lifetime income at a time when you may be concerned about the future of the economy and the investment markets.

11 MAKING THE RIGHT STOCK INVESTMENTS

The stock market scares the daylights out of me. At one point my stock investments lost half their value. I've read that it's too late to sell, but I wonder if it makes any sense to hold on to my stocks and stock funds with the economy in such a pickle. Some investment managers are even recommending that people buy stock. Are they crazy or what?

The year 2008 will be remembered as the year when the old guidelines about investing in the stock market, like "buy and hold," and "stocks always beat bonds," became anathema to investors. At one point in late 2008, many stock indexes had declined over 50 percent, and very few experts could conjure up any optimism for stocks until there were clear signs that the myriad solutions thrown at the credit crisis were starting to work. No wonder investors are asking: Is there any reason to hold stocks until the economy improves? Isn't the economy going to get worse before it gets better?

This chapter will help bring some sanity to the hysteria surrounding stock market investing, about which more opinions are expressed than there are stocks to trade. The stock investors who are or will be most affected by events that only come around a couple of times a century fall into two categories: first, those who overreact to market adversity by making quick decisions to shift major portions of their investments, and second, those who are paralyzed into inaction in response to sudden and significant changes in market conditions, which can be as detrimental as overreacting.

Even investors who choose to maintain a steady course in the face of market uncertainty are confused by the conflicting opinions of investment managers. Everyone has an opinion about the stock market, and no two experts agree. Some of the most respected names in the investment business, all successful money managers, provided the following opinions in one week in late 2008.

- Don't buy stocks for the next three years.
- Stock valuations haven't been this attractive for decades.
- The recent rally will continue. This week will be particularly strong, since buyers who are afraid to miss the rebound will be snapping up stocks. (The Dow Jones Industrial Average declined 4 percent that week.)
- The key to avoiding losses in stocks is to buy stocks on Monday and sell them on Thursday.
- The worst is over, and the stock market is poised for a quick rally of 30 to 50 percent.
- Our models show that stocks will go nowhere over the next 10 to 15 years.

HISTORY LESSON

While you may never want to own a share of stock ever again, you'll probably come back to the fold. After all, stocks dropped by half during the 2000–2002 bear market, but investors' appetite for stocks was whetted soon thereafter. Here's why it's always important to own stocks in all markets. The table that follows shows stock performance at the end of every recession over the past 60 years. It shows the gains in both the year the recession ended and the year after the recession ended. That's important, because since the stock market is always looking to the future, it doesn't wait around for the recession to end to begin regaining its losses. In fact, if the consistent patterns of past recessions are any indicator, if you wait to replenish your stock holdings until the economists declare that the recession has officially ended, you will miss a big portion of the gain.

Out of Weakness . . . Strength: Postrecession Stock Market Gains*

Past Recessions	Duration	Year Recession Ended	Year after Recession Ended
1953–1954	1 year	+53%	32%
1957–1958	1 year	+43%	12%
1973–1975	2 years	+37%	24%
1980–1982	2 years	+21%	22%
1990–1991	1 year	+31%	8%
2001–2003	2 years	+29%	11%

*Standard & Poor's 500 Stock Index.

SUGGESTIONS FOR BECOMING A SAVVY STOCK INVESTOR

Here are suggestions for making the most of your stock and stock mutual fund investments in the worst economic environment since the Great Depression.

Patience and Discipline

Successful stock investing requires patience and discipline, and the next couple of years will test these attributes sorely. After enduring big drops in stock prices across the board, the temptation to cash out is overwhelming at times. The idea of buying stocks in such a market makes you wonder if you've lost your mind. Patience and discipline are also important attributes for your investment advisor. You should expect no less.

Establish a Stock Investing Plan and Stick to It

When the stock market is volatile and trending downward, it's natural to think that it's too late to do anything, so just let the investment gods take over. That's not a plan. Rather, a plan should look out five or ten years, a period of time that includes a stock market recovery. While your plan may be to ride out the storm with the investments you already own, that's okay as long as you think it through. Once you or your advisor makes a plan, don't abandon it. While you might want to make some sensible midcourse adjustments, they should not deviate significantly from your plan. Consistency pays.

Shun Those Who Think They Can Predict the Future of the Stock Market

There will always be people who think they can predict the future of the investment markets. Those who do either have an agenda (they want to sell you something or promote their firm) or, more likely, they are delusional and should therefore be shunned. It's impossible to predict with complete accuracy how the investment markets will fare, particularly over the near future. But just as bad as following the fantastical and fallacious forecast of a single person is following the crowd. It was the crowd mentality that bid up the dot.com stocks back in the late 1990s and caused investors to overdose on stocks during the 2003–2007 bull market.

Here is a technique that will almost certainly keep you out of trouble: do the opposite of what the crowd is doing. In other words, lighten up on stocks when the mob is euphoric and buy when it's morose. This is very, very difficult to do at any time, particularly when the market is in free fall, but you'll probably be better off financially if you can muster the courage to do so. Here's a case in point: Warren Buffett, arguably the greatest investor on the planet, started buying stocks in early 2008, when the stock market began to weaken. Then the market plummeted, and some supposed experts said that Buffett had lost his touch. But he kept adding to his holdings as the stock market was sinking. Here's a question. Five years from now, who do you think will be correct? The pundits who said that Buffett had lost his touch or Buffett?

Size Does Matter

Stocks are often classified according to the size of the company as measured by the total value of its stock: large company, mid-sized company, and small company. Large-company stocks have been holding up better than small-company stocks amidst the sharp decline in stock prices. But over the long term, small- and midsized-company stocks usually outperform, so every well-diversified portfolio should include stocks in all three categories. If you like to own shares of individual companies, stick with large companies. It's too risky to buy individual shares of smaller and midsized companies, so the smartest way to own them is through so-called small-cap and mid-cap mutual funds or exchange-traded funds.

Go Global

There is a lot more to stock investing than buying U.S. stocks. In fact, U.S. stocks historically have not performed as well as foreign stocks, although that has not been the case recently, as foreign economies are suffering even more than the United States amidst the global economic crisis. But that doesn't make foreign stocks any less attractive. The only feasible way to play the foreign markets is to buy a good international mutual fund. Avoid single-country funds or single-region funds. Look for garden variety international funds that scour the world for the best investment opportunities in countries with advanced economies and thriving stock markets. To round out your international holdings, also consider owning an "emerging markets" mutual fund that invests in rapidly growing developing countries like China and India.

Buy and Hold No Longer Works

The days when you could buy some stocks and stock funds and hold onto them indefinitely are gone. Actually, those days are long gone. Since the beginning of this decade, you could no longer rely on a previously reliable investment serving you well indefinitely. The ups and downs of the stock market are at all-time highs, and this can affect even the bluest of blue chip stocks and the most consistent mutual fund. You or your investment advisor needs to review your individual stock holdings regularly. Consider weeding out any companies with poor prospects in this difficult economy. Plenty of companies have poor prospects. Also review your mutual funds. Some of the all-time best mutual funds stumbled horribly during the recent stock market crash. If you have a mutual fund whose performance is deteriorating compared with the average for its peer group (for example, your small-cap fund is badly underperforming the average small-cap fund), replace it with a better performer.

Safe Money Checklist

Making the Right Stock Investments

✔ If you significantly reduced your stock holdings, don't wait for the recession's end to get back in.

✔ Patience and discipline will serve you well during and after the current market turmoil.

✔ Establish a stock investing plan now and stick to it.

✔ Rely on those who predict the future of the stock market at your own peril.

✔ Including small-company and international stock funds will better diversify your stock holdings.

✔ Buying and holding stock investments indefinitely is no longer an effective strategy. Review your individual stock and stock fund holdings regularly.

---

12 Making the Right Bond Investments

I have always invested primarily in bank accounts and CDs. While that has saved me from the recent declines in the stock market, I've never made very much interest on my money. I realize that I need to get comfortable with stocks, but my parents say I could earn more interest on bonds. I'm not familiar with them, but I still think you can lose money on bonds.

Corporate bonds, municipal bonds, Ginnie Maes, Treasury Inflation-Protected Securities (TIPS), I bonds—when it comes to making bond investments, it is easy to get confused. The one thing these investments have in common is that they all pay interest. Beyond that, there can be significant differences, which I will explain. There are so many choices that finding the right investment is difficult, even in prosperous times. When the future of the economy is uncertain, it is difficult even for the experts to get a handle on the direction of interest rates, and finding the right bond investment becomes even more difficult.

Bonds and/or bond mutual funds belong in every well-diversified investment portfolio. If you doubt that, ask anyone who had all of her money in stocks at the beginning of 2008 for her opinion about bonds. Bonds are part of the foundation of a solid investment portfolio. While bonds can fluctuate in value like stocks, they generally don't fluctuate as much, and the interest they pay provides a steady addition to portfolio values as well as income for investors who need income, notably retirees.

On the surface, bond investing is pretty straightforward, with two basic objectives: to earn interest and to get your principal back when you sell the bonds. The economic downturn adds considerable complexity to the evaluation of the investments you own, as well as new investments. For example, no one knows what will happen to interest rates as the massive worldwide bailout progresses. Many factors could influence interest rates, including oil prices, the depth of the recession, and actions by the federal government to get the U.S. economy back on track, replete with trillion-dollar budget deficits. You also have to consider the safety of your bond investments, especially since many sectors of the economy are in serious trouble, and numerous cor-

porations and even some municipal governments will be default-
ing on their bonds.

A SMORGASBORD OF CHOICE

Before delving into bonds, a little explanation is in order. There
are two categories of interest-earning investments. One is bonds,
and the other is temporary investments, or, more formally, cash-
equivalent investments. These are interest-earning securities that
can be converted into cash at any time with little or no change
in principal value. In other words, you get your principal (your
original investment) back—no more and no less—when you sell,
plus you receive interest along the way. Temporary investments
include money market accounts (sold by banks) and money market funds (sold by mutual funds), Treasury bills, savings accounts,
and other such investments. While the principal doesn't fluctuate, the interest paid on temporary investments does. Temporary
investments are discussed in Chapter 14.

Bonds are also called fixed-income investments. "Fixed
income" means that the interest rate on the investment remains
the same, or is fixed, regardless of what happens to overall interest rates. However, the value of your principal will change with
the prevailing interest rates. In essence, bond values decline if
interest rates rise and vice versa. Bonds have a maturity date,
which is the date on which you get the bond's principal back.
Some of the many available fixed-income investments are Treasury notes and bonds; mortgage-backed securities, such as Ginnie Maes; government-sponsored enterprise (GSE) securities,
like Federal Farm Credit Bank and Federal Home Loan Bank
bonds; municipal bonds; and corporate bonds.

You can buy bonds or temporary investments directly by buying individual securities through banks or stockbrokers, or indirectly through a mutual fund where you own a portion of a diversified portfolio of bonds or temporary investments.

BALANCING RISK AND RETURN WITH YOUR BOND INVESTMENTS

No matter what your financial circumstances, interest-rate outlook, or comfort with investment risk, there are appropriate bond investments for you.

Buy Quality

Although there is no agreement on the outlook for interest rates, the experts do agree that in the current economic climate, you should concentrate on high-quality bond investments such as Treasury securities, certificates of deposit from federally insured banks, and high-grade corporate and municipal bonds. If you invest in bond mutual funds, opt for funds that emphasize high-quality securities.

Diversify

The worse the economy gets, the more important it is to diversify. Unless you have only a very small amount of money to invest, don't concentrate your bond investments in a single or very few securities. Select several different issues and different bond categories: government, corporate, and municipal bonds, for example. The easiest way to diversify is to own bond mutual funds.

Ladder Maturities

One of the best ways to hedge your bets in an uncertain interest-rate environment is to ladder bond maturities—in other words, purchase bonds with differing maturities, for example, one, three, five, and seven years. That way, if interest rates rise, you'll have a bond coming due to reinvest at the higher rates. You don't have to place a heavy bet on a single maturity. You can ladder maturities with bond mutual funds by owning short-, intermediate-, and long-term bond funds.

Keep Maturities Short

While long-maturity bond investments usually pay higher interest rates than shorter-maturity investments, there may not be enough of a difference to justify the greater risks in longer-term investing. Too much uncertainty surrounds the economy and the possibility of inflation or even deflation, at least until the worldwide credit crisis is resolved. Therefore, most experts suggest keeping investment maturities on individual bonds that you own rather short, generally less than 10 years.

Seek Safe Harbors if You Expect the Worst

Many investors are scared about the prospects for the economy, given the number of bankruptcies, bailouts (which are just Band-Aids hiding massive problems in many financial companies), and dismal economic and corporate profit outlooks. If you count yourself among the skeptics, stick with short-term, no-risk bonds and temporary investments. On the bond side, short-maturity U.S. Treasury notes and short-term bond funds that invest in Treasury securities are the safest. (Note: a "note" is the equivalent of a short-term bond.)

WHICH BONDS MAKE SENSE FOR YOU?

I think we can all agree that this is no time to speculate with bonds. Whether the bond issuer is a corporation, a state government, or a municipality, most are suffering financially. There is a distinct possibility that some, if not many, issuers will become unable to meet their debt obligations. You can lose a lot of money with seemingly safe bonds just as fast as you can with stocks.

The best indicator of just how dire the situation may be is the heavy demand for the safest of all debt issues, U.S. Treasury securities. High demand drives down the interest paid on a bond, and in late 2008, the interest paid by U.S. Treasury securities reached an all-time low. Here are some thoughts about the prospects for the major bond categories.

U.S. Government Securities

These are the safest place for your money, but don't expect to get paid very much interest, particularly from U.S. Treasuries. Nevertheless, if you think there is no end in sight for the many problems plaguing the U.S. and world economies, you'll sleep better with Treasury securities. Other U.S. government securities offer security and generally pay more interest than Treasuries. U.S. TIPS pay a small rate of interest plus additional interest that tracks the rate of inflation. You can get a similar inflation kicker with I Series U.S. Savings Bonds. Bond issues of the Government National Mortgage Association (Ginnie Mae) may also be attractive, as may those issued by GSEs, including Federal Farm Credit Bank and Federal Home Loan Bank securities, which usually pay higher interest than U.S. Treasuries.

While you can be comfortable knowing that you'll receive interest as well as get your principal back with U.S. government securities, as with all bonds, they can lose value if interest rates rise and you (or the mutual fund manager, if the money is in a fund) sell the securities before they mature.

Corporate Bonds

Corporate bonds have been and will probably continue to be the category most affected by the stricken economy. Despite the high interest paid by many corporate bonds, this is not an area for money that you want to keep safe. Even big companies with high debt ratings have recently run into big trouble. On the other hand, because of slackening demand for corporate bonds, the interest paid on them is considerably higher than what you can fetch from U.S. government securities. If you'd like to take some risk for the opportunity to earn higher interest, the most prudent way to do so would be to buy a corporate bond mutual fund. But stick to funds that invest in higher-quality corporate bonds. Unless you have a big appetite for risk, avoid high-yield (junk) bond funds.

Municipal Bonds

Municipal bonds are very attractive, although investors must consider the risk that at least some governments may have difficulty meeting their obligations to pay interest and to repay principal at maturity. The fiscal situation in many municipalities and several states is dire, so your portfolio should include many different individual issues and only the highest-quality municipal bonds. Don't put much faith in insured municipal bonds. The municipal bond insurers are themselves victims of the subprime mortgage crisis, and their ability to make good on the debt of failed municipalities cannot be assured.

The interest paid on municipal bonds and municipal bond funds is as attractive as it has been in a generation. These bonds have been paying higher interest rates than U.S. Treasury notes and bonds, which is highly unusual since, while Treasury interest is subject to federal income tax, municipal bonds are exempt from federal taxes. This means that after taxes have been factored in, municipals are paying much higher interest than Treasuries. Munis are therefore well worth a look, because rates won't stay this high forever. If you're in the market for individual bond issues, my recommendation is to stick with high-quality muni bonds backed by projects that are not likely to suffer unduly if the state's finances are strained. Examples include bonds supporting educational facilities and essential services like water and sewer.

Of course, owning a municipal bond mutual fund will address the quality and diversity challenges of a single bond investment, but avoid high-yield municipal bond funds for the same reason that you should avoid high-yield corporate bond funds. This is no time to be investing in shaky borrowers.

Foreign Bonds

If you think the U.S. economy is on life support, it's nothing compared with the situation in many foreign countries. Add to that the great uncertainty about how the U.S. dollar will fare against foreign currencies, and you quickly come to the conclusion that foreign bonds should be avoided until there are clear signs that the world economies are well on the road back to health.

Safe Money Checklist

Making the Right Bond Investments

✔ Bonds or bond mutual funds belong in every well-diversified investment portfolio.

✔ Try not to limit your bond investments to a single type of bond. There are probably several different categories of bond investments that are appropriate for you.

✔ Stick to high-quality bonds and bond funds; avoid junk bond funds.

✔ Hedge your bets by laddering the maturities on your bonds.

✔ If you are particularly pessimistic about the economy, stick with U.S. government securities.

✔ Take advantage of unusually attractive municipal bond yields by investing in high-quality municipal bonds and municipal bond funds.

13 MAKING THE RIGHT REAL ESTATE INVESTMENTS

This real estate market looks too luscious to pass up. The auction notices in the newspaper fill up two pages, and I heard that the local banks are holding a bunch of foreclosed properties that they're dying to get rid of. It looks like the perfect time to buy a couple of properties for a song.

Real estate has traditionally been one of the best ways for people of average means to get rich. But, as many real estate investors have found out and will continue to find out during the Great Recession, it is also possible to lose a lot of money. If you own real estate, you may be troubled by the deterioration of the real estate market. If you are a potential real estate buyer, you may be tempted by the apparent bargains flooding the market. This chapter will provide some guidance for people who already own, or are interested in purchasing, investment real estate in a perilous market. Advice for homeowners, as opposed to real estate investors, appears in Chapter 20, and opportunities for home buyers are reviewed in Chapter 22.

BLEAK REAL ESTATE OUTLOOK

The outlook for investment real estate in 2009 and 2010 is bleak. Vacancies are rising in most areas as many chain stores close their doors, and the home market is flooded with foreclosed properties. Loan money to help sustain beleaguered property owners is hard to come by. Mortgage defaults by large and small real estate investors alike are expected to continue for several years.

THE THREE WAYS TO INVEST IN REAL ESTATE

Despite the dour outlook, real estate investing can play an important role in a well-diversified investment portfolio. Real estate is considered the fourth major investment category, after stocks (Chapter 11), bonds (Chapter 12), and temporary investments (Chapter 14). Many people choose not to invest in real estate, and this is perfectly okay. If you are interested in real estate investing, there are three ways to participate.

1. **Real estate stocks.** The fancy term for a real estate stock is a real estate investment trust (REIT). A REIT is a corporation that invests in real estate or mortgages and whose shares trade on the stock exchange, so for no more than the cost of buying some shares of stock, you can participate in the real estate market.

2. **Real estate mutual funds.** Just as a stock mutual fund invests in a lot of individual stocks, a real estate mutual fund invests in a gaggle of individual REITs. Just as with a garden variety mutual fund, real estate funds diversify your money so that it is protected somewhat in the event that one or a few REIT stocks plummet. You can choose an actively managed real estate fund or a real estate exchange-traded fund or index fund that replicates a real estate index.

3. **Individual properties.** Of the three ways to own real estate, purchasing it yourself provides the greatest returns—and the greatest risks. There are two types of own-it-yourself real estate. *Income-producing real estate* can range from a rented home or condominium unit to an apartment building, to commercial property. If you purchase wisely— in other words, if you don't overpay for the property—you can enjoy good cash flow, possible tax benefits, and significant long-term appreciation in value. Most people, however, lack the time, the resources, or the inclination to manage income-producing real estate. *Undeveloped land* ties up a lot of money, often for a long time. Land in particularly desirable areas is very expensive, but with some luck it will appreciate handsomely in value, and it doesn't necessitate the hassles of managing a property.

ADVICE FOR REAL ESTATE INVESTORS

Here are some thoughts on the type of real estate investment that might make the best sense for you.

- **REIT stocks.** Investors who are interested in fat dividends, particularly retirees, are often attracted to individual REIT stocks. Given the troubled outlook, however, REIT investors should be aware that dividends may be reduced. Also, rather than concentrating on one or two REIT stocks, you should spread your money around among several issues in the event that some REITs get into financial trouble.

- **Real estate mutual funds.** Given the uncertainty surrounding the real estate sector, real estate mutual funds, whose managers work full time analyzing the real estate industry and individual REITs, are the preferred way to invest. While the outlook for real estate in general is not very bright, that doesn't necessarily mean that you should avoid putting some money into a real estate fund. Real estate will return to its prior glory, and you want to be a participant when it starts to revive.

  While most real estate funds invest in U.S. properties, a growing number invest part or all of their money in overseas real estate. As the worldwide economy revives, many foreign countries will boom once again, so investing in an international real estate fund will allow you to participate in the rapid growth overseas.

- **Individual properties.** Slumping real estate prices are attracting experienced and first-time real estate investors alike. But this is not an investment to be taken lightly, despite the infomercials that make buying and managing real estate look so easy—and cheap. If you would like to at least consider investing in real estate, see the following discussion. Also, Chapter 22 has some suggestions for buying distressed homes.

WANT TO OWN A PROPERTY?

Despite the many pitfalls, owning individual properties can be an excellent investment. True, being a landlord is no picnic, but a lot of people don't seem to mind it. However, you have to avoid overpaying. Even amidst a depressed real estate market, finding a worthwhile property is very difficult.

Rule of Thumb

If you're ever considering a property, the "rent multiplier" is an easy calculation that you can make to decide if the property is reasonably priced. Here's the rule: any property selling for much more than seven times the total annual rental is likely to yield a negative cash flow; in other words, your rental income won't be sufficient to cover your mortgage and operating expenses, let alone make a profit. To determine the rent multiplier, which compares the total selling price with the current gross annual rental, use the following formula:

$$\text{Rent multiplier} = \frac{\text{Selling price}}{\text{Total annual rent income}}$$

Example

The asking price of a single-family home is $180,000, and it generates $12,000 in annual rent. The rent multiplier is calculated as follows:

$$\text{Rent multiplier} = \frac{\text{Selling price}}{\text{Total annual rent income}} = \frac{\$180,000}{\$12,000} = 15 \text{ times rental}$$

The property is selling for 15 times the annual rental, way over the limit of 7 times annual rental. In order for a property earning $12,000 per year in rent to be a worthwhile investment, you should pay no more than $84,000 for the property ($12,000 rent times 7). That's why, even with current depressed real estate prices, it's very difficult to buy a reasonably priced condo or single-family home. Apartments or small commercial properties might work, but they require a lot more money up front. Incidentally, professional real estate investors generally won't pay more than five to six times gross annual rental.

Undeveloped Land

If the notion of managing a property is not your cup of tea, you could consider investing in undeveloped land, also called raw land. Good undeveloped land is expensive and hard to finance over more than a few years. Also, it doesn't bring in any income, so it can tie up a lot of money for a long time. But well-situated land can have tremendous price appreciation potential.

Here's an idea: if you think you may want to relocate to a different area of the country, perhaps after you retire, or that you may want to purchase a second home somewhere in the future, put a stake in the ground by purchasing a top-notch building lot or small land parcel in that area. If you decide to relocate there and housing prices in the area have skyrocketed, your land will have kept up with price increases. If you decide not to live or vacation there, you're still probably holding an excellent investment.

Safe Money Checklist

Making the Right Real Estate Investments

✔ Real estate investments usually play a role in a well-diversified portfolio.

✔ Owning a real estate mutual fund is the easiest way to own real estate.

✔ Owning individual properties is risky, but it can be very rewarding financially.

✔ The rent multiplier is an easy way to determine whether a contemplated property is attractively priced.

14 KEEPING SAFE MONEY SAFE

I've got some money sitting in a savings account earning only 1 percent interest. I want to keep the money safe, but there's got to be a better alternative.

The problems in the investment markets have been so pervasive that even some previously safe investments have become risky. There are a lot of reasons why everyone should have at least some of his money invested in securities without having to worry about the money losing value or suddenly becoming inaccessible, including:

- To meet foreseeable short-term cash needs that can't be paid for out of your job income, like college tuition, home improvements, a car, or some other big-ticket item.

- Even if you don't foresee any cash needs, it's often helpful to have at least a few months' living expenses safely tucked away, because we all know that unanticipated costs inevitably arise, particularly when the economy reeks.
- To temporarily take some money off the stock and bond table if the markets are so scary that you're beginning to have nightmares featuring you receiving an employee of the month certificate at a fast-food emporium—when you're 85.
- To gradually invest a substantial amount of money. Perhaps you or your investment advisor has already moved a lot of money out of stocks, bonds, and mutual funds to the proverbial "sidelines." If so, you want to make sure that the money is both safe and accessible. Despite your understandable distaste for "risky" investments, you will eventually want to gradually get back in the game. In the meantime, though, you want your sideline money to be safe and accessible.
- When you retire, you might also want to keep enough of your retirement investments in safe securities to fund up to two years' worth of living expenses. This will prevent you from having to sell other investments at a loss in a down market.

THE SAFE MONEY THREE-STEP

The investment industry offers several safe money alternatives under the umbrella of "short-term investments," "temporary investments," or, in Wall Street jargon, "cash-equivalent invest-ments," or just plain "cash." Whatever you call them, these alter-natives have two things in common: they pay interest, and there is little or no risk that you'll lose principal. With a couple of exceptions, you can also take your money out immediately with no loss of principal. These are the three essentials that need to be considered when deciding where to put your safe money:

1. **Safe.** Whether you are fleeing the stock market or temporarily setting money aside to be used in the near future, you don't want to risk losing your principal.
2. **Accessible.** You want to be able to get your hands on the money within a day, ideally at no cost or minimal cost.
3. **Decent interest.** You want to earn an attractive rate of interest. Since the interest rate paid on safe investments varies considerably, doing some comparison shopping will be rewarding.

INVESTMENT CHOICES

Here is a rundown of various safe money investment choices with my admittedly somewhat biased opinions.

Available through Banks or Credit Unions
- **Savings accounts.** These are federally insured, but they usually pay pitifully low interest rates.
- **Money market deposit accounts.** These are federally insured, but usually pay low interest rates, although some institutions offer returns that are competitive with brokerage money market funds.

Available through Mutual Funds or Brokers
- **General money market funds.** Usually these pay the highest interest among money market funds, but investors

who are concerned about safety might opt for government or Treasury money market funds. The federal government has provided some money market fund guarantees to participating fund companies and brokerage firms, but only for money that was in the fund as of September 19, 2008. The guarantees are temporary. Check with your investment company to see if it is participating.

- **Government money market funds.** These are considered safer than general money market funds, but you pay for the additional safety with a lower yield.
- **U.S. Treasury money market funds.** These are the safest money market funds, but the interest paid is likely to be rock bottom.
- **Tax-exempt money market funds.** Interest is exempt from federal income taxes, so high-tax-bracket investors might benefit.
- **Single-state tax-exempt money market funds.** Interest is exempt from both federal and state income taxes, but be wary of unusually high yields, as this may be an indication of state fiscal problems.

Available through Banks or Brokers
- **U.S. Treasury bills.** These are ultra safe, but the interest paid may be almost nonexistent. In late 2008, a $10,000 investment in a three-month Treasury bill would have earned a mere 25 cents in interest. If a T-bill is not held to maturity, you may suffer a small loss of principal.
- **Certificates of deposit (CDs).** These are federally insured, and they are also available from credit unions. They are likely to provide the best interest rate among

safe investments, although you should always compare CD rates against other alternatives. An interest penalty will be assessed if the CD is sold before maturity.

One of the unfortunate outcomes of declining investment markets and low interest rates is that some investors are suckered into putting money in what they are told are safe investments that pay inordinately high interest. Don't take the bait. Stick with familiar investments.

Finding the Best Returns

Compared with stocks and bonds, safe investments are pretty straightforward. The price you pay for safety and liquidity is a lower rate of interest than that paid by bonds and other longer-term investments. And while cash-equivalent investments hardly offer breathtaking returns, you might as well earn as much as you can on them. With a little bit of effort, you can make the most of these otherwise mundane investments. Here are some suggestions:

- **Shop for a CD.** If you're in the market for a CD, a little shopping around—even outside your hometown—could reap some rewards. First compare rates among banks in town. If you have a broker, check with her about CD offerings that the brokerage firm may have. Finally, several Web sites, including www.bankrate.com, list the highest-yielding CDs in the country. Remember, as long as the issuing bank is FDIC insured (or, if the CD is offered by a credit union, is backed by credit union insurance), you really shouldn't care where your CD comes from. You just want the best yield. If you're concerned about how your CD and other bank accounts could be affected by a bank failure, see Chapter 8.

- **Compare money market fund yields.** If you have an account with a mutual fund or a broker offering several different kinds of money market funds, be sure to compare yields to make sure the one you select offers the best *after-tax* return as long as you're comfortable that the money fund meets your safety requirements. This may require you to periodically compare the returns among various money market funds, but, hey, if you can improve your return by periodically switching among money market funds, it's more money in your pocket.

- **Save on Treasury bill purchases.** Although current convoluted market conditions have driven Treasury bill yields way down, this won't last forever. If you regularly buy T-bills, consider buying them directly from the U.S. Treasury at no cost. Simply visit www.treasurydirect.com for information and applications for buying Treasury securities online. If you don't want to go through the effort of buying T-bills online directly from the Fed, compare fees between your bank and your brokerage firm.

Safe Money Checklist

Keeping Money Safe

✔ Money that is temporarily on the sidelines is best put into securities that are both safe and accessible.

✔ Compare the many safe money investment alternatives to find those categories that are paying the best interest consistent with your needs for safety and accessibility.

✔ Once you have decided on a safe money category (money market fund or CD, for example), comparison-shop to identify those that pay the best interest within that category.

Part IV

Tackling Special Situations

15 If You Lose Your Job

I lost my job yesterday after 11 years at the company.
I was tempted not to tell my family last night, but I did.
I just don't know how we're going to make it financially.

Losing your job is traumatic under any circumstances, but particularly when unemployment is high and job prospects seem bleak. Vast numbers of American workers are being laid off, at the rate of over 50,000 *per week* in late 2008, with most economists predicting that the number of layoffs will grow even more in 2009. If you've recently joined the ranks of the unemployed, you need to attend to two very important but difficult matters. First, you must strive to overcome the personal anxiety you almost certainly are experiencing. Second, you need to assess your financial situation, so that you can cope with the loss of income. Above all, don't panic. You *can* and *will* overcome this temporary setback.

OVERCOMING ANXIETY

You must overcome the inevitable psychological and emotional stress. Most people go through three stages of anxiety.

1. **The *immediate panic* associated with the loss of employment.** Your first reaction may be to hide this fact from your family and friends. Some people even go to the extreme of leaving home every day as if they were going to their job. Avoid this temptation. Your family and friends will provide enormous support, and the more support you have, the easier it will be for you to get back on your feet and find another, probably better, job.

2. **Guilt and lack of self-worth.** After your initial panic has subsided, you may begin to blame yourself for your plight. You may feel that you have let yourself and your family down, and be convinced that job prospects are going to be pretty poor. Obviously, these feelings are not going to help your situation, but you need to recognize that you are likely to go through this stage.

3. **Anger at the world.** Finally, you will begin to feel angry about your situation, and it is not until you get through this last stage that you will be in the frame of mind to present yourself to a prospective employer convincingly. This stage typically leads to renewed self-confidence and determination.

Most important, you must be willing to ask for help. Other people can offer emotional support and can be a source of information about new employment opportunities. The sooner you face up to your situation, the sooner you will be able to evaluate your financial situation, and the sooner you will be able to begin the search for a new job.

Coping with the Loss of Income

In spite of the emotional trauma, you must evaluate your current financial situation realistically, so that you can adjust to your temporarily changed financial circumstances. This is particularly important because you have lost your job during a recession, and therefore, you may spend more time unemployed than you would during more prosperous times. You need to address the following matters.

- **Understanding severance benefits.** Be sure you understand your employer's severance benefits, such as salary continuation, payment for accrued vacation, and insurance benefits. If you are about to be laid off or have just been laid off, it may be possible to negotiate additional severance benefits from your employer. Experts suggest that this be done within a day or two of the layoff, when the employer is most apt to respond to your appeal. (See Chapter 16.)
- **Assuring the continuation of health and life insurance coverage.** It is advantageous to continue to carry your employer-provided health and life insurance coverage, as well as any other insurance coverage that your employer offers and will allow you to continue. Most employers are required by law to allow you to continue your company health insurance plan for up to 18 months (or longer in some circumstances) without a medical checkup, as long as you pay the premiums. While the premiums may be

steep, you should not go one minute without health insurance coverage. Alternatively, you might be able to save some money by purchasing a temporary insurance policy, which usually covers periods from three months to one year. Acquiring a new policy, even a temporary one, may require a medical checkup and/or preclude preexisting conditions. Be sure that the temporary health insurance coverage does not leave any gaps that could cost you dearly when you can least afford it.

If your employer does not continue your life insurance coverage, you may be able to convert your employer's group policy to an individual policy. Otherwise, you may be able to purchase low-cost life insurance coverage to replace your company-provided policy by shopping around for the best rates. See Chapter 8 for tips on acquiring and maintaining adequate insurance coverage when times are tough.

- **Applying for unemployment compensation benefits.** If you've been let go, you are entitled to collect unemployment compensation benefits. Strange as it may seem, some people, perhaps out of a sense of pride or out of embarrassment, don't want to collect these benefits, even though they are eligible. By all means apply for unemployment compensation as soon as you lose your job.

- **Summarizing your ready resources.** Almost everyone is suffering from the current economic downturn, and if you are recently unemployed, you are doubly affected. Your primary financial concern is how you're going to meet your financial obligations during your unemployment period, so you should begin by summarizing your ready resources—cash that is now available, as well as any investments that can be sold in a short period of time. The following table will help you summarize your ready resources. Once you know how much or how little you have available, you can begin to prepare a budget that will sustain you during a period of unemployment.

Summary of Ready Resources

Cash in bank accounts	$_____
Savings, money market accounts	_____
CDs and other interest-earning investments	_____
Stock investments	_____
Mutual funds	_____
Other resources available	_____
Total ready resources	$_____

- **Reducing spending.** Unless you are one of the few who are blessed with abundant ready resources, you are probably going to have to reduce your spending, at least for a while. Before you can do this, you should summarize your past spending patterns so that you can identify ways to cut expenses.
- **Preparing a budget.** Once you have figured out what income and resources you have ready and how you have been spending your money, you are ready to prepare a budget, which ideally should ensure that you will be able to meet important bills over the next six months. First, you should project your income, including any severance

benefits, unemployment benefits, income from your spouse's or partner's job, and investment income, unless you will have to liquidate those investments to meet living expenses. Next, summarize your expected expenses, starting with the expenses that must be paid—rent/mortgage, insurance, and groceries, for example—and ending with those expenses that can be forgone, such as dining out and vacations. After you have summarized your projected expenses, you can compare them with your expected income and decide how you are going to close the gap between income (probably too little) and expenses (probably too much). The key to dealing with the financial strain of unemployment is to reduce expenses as much as possible, and if your unemployment income is insufficient to meet your reduced expense level, as it probably will be, you will have to use ready resources to help meet expenses.

Here are a few other tips:

- Keep up with your mortgage payments, since your house is probably your largest investment. Chapter 20 includes comments on what to do if you fall behind on your mortgage payments.
- You may be able to borrow from your or your spouse's or partner's company retirement savings [401(k) or 403(b)] plans or pension plan. But tapping into these important retirement plans should not be taken lightly.
- Other retirement accounts, such as IRAs and deferred annuities, can also be tapped, although you'll probably incur hefty taxes and a penalty.

- Consider part-time work to augment your income. You'll be surprised at how much part-time work may be available, even during a severe recession.
- Weigh carefully the temptation that many laid-off people have of starting their own business. See Chapter 26 for more guidance.
- If it appears likely that you are going to have trouble meeting your obligations to creditors, be sure to contact them to try to work out a more comfortable payment schedule. See Chapter 19 for more information on dealing with creditors when times are tough.
- The sooner you get to work conducting a job search, the better. See Chapter 18.

Safe Money Checklist

If You Lose Your Job

✔ Above all, don't panic. You will survive this setback, just as you have survived and will survive the other setbacks we all experience during our lifetimes. Accept the fact that you are going to experience a lot of stress, particularly right after you lose your job. Seek and welcome the support of your family and friends.

✔ Take advantage of unemployment compensation benefits that you are entitled to.

✔ Continue or replace all important employer-provided insurance coverage. Continue paying the premiums on your other insurance policies.

✔ Summarize the resources you have available to meet living expenses during the period of unemployment.

✔ Budget carefully for the future by analyzing your past spending patterns, determining ways you can cut back on expenses, and figuring out where you are going to obtain sufficient resources.

✔ Begin your job search quickly and enthusiastically.

16 If You Think You Might Lose Your Job

My company is having a terrible time with the worldwide economic meltdown. We rely a lot on foreign buyers. The company hasn't laid anybody off yet, but rumors are circulating that it may soon. My area may be vulnerable to a layoff if one does come, and I don't have much seniority. Things are hard enough right now with the way the economy is going, but I don't even want to think about what will happen if I lose my job.

It's perfectly natural to worry about a layoff. After all, the news reports of huge layoffs and frightening unemployment statistics hardly inspire confidence. If you are one of the many people who fear that they may lose their job because of the current economic crisis or for some other reason, you should start planning now. Even if you don't lose your job, you won't be any worse off for making these preparations. Preparing in advance for the loss of a job can reduce the disruptions to your career and personal finances that are almost inevitable if you become unemployed.

EVALUATING YOUR JOB STATUS

Assess the Situation

Perhaps the first thing to do if you are worried about losing your job is to assess, as realistically as possible, the probability that this might happen. Rumors of massive layoffs can circulate around some large companies for years without any layoffs actually occurring. Many more people fret about being laid off than actually join the ranks of the unemployed. While these economic times make it more difficult to speculate on company layoffs, you still should try to make an objective assessment of the likelihood that you are going to lose your job and when it might occur. Has the company gone through previous layoffs? How essential is your department, and how is it doing during the recession?

Examine Job Opportunities

Should you look for another job? If your assessment leads you to believe that you may be one of the victims, you may not want to wait for the ax to fall. Since current economic conditions make job hunting even more difficult than it is normally, you may benefit by beginning your job search now, but do it discreetly, of course.

Arm Yourself with Information

Another advantage of being realistic about your job prospects is that you can prepare for the fateful day, not only from a financial standpoint, which is discussed later in this chapter, but also from the standpoint of dealing with your employer. Even though most layoff victims anticipate that they are going to lose their jobs, they are often so shocked when the time comes that they are not in a position to negotiate a better severance arrangement. Your employer is much more likely to accommodate your needs if you express them immediately at the time of severance. Experts suggest that you will be able to do this much better if you are prepared for the layoff. Remember, the company is as uncomfortable about letting people go as the employees are about being let go. Even if you are not in a position to improve your severance arrangement, by being mentally prepared, you will be well on your way to landing on your feet and finding another job.

REVIEW YOUR FINANCIAL STATUS

You can take several financial actions prior to your expected unemployment that can help reduce your fiscal duress. Incidentally, many of these suggestions are a good idea under any circumstances, not just under threat of imminent unemployment.

Prepare a Survival Budget

You should prepare a budget that assumes that you will be unemployed for a period of six months, or even more if you are a highly compensated executive. First, estimate your income during unemployment, including unemployment compensation benefits and severance payments. Look carefully at your past expenses, and classify them according to expenses that must be paid (such as the mortgage or rent and insurance), necessities that could be reduced somewhat in the event of dire financial straits, and discretionary expenses like clothing, vacations, and meals at restaurants. Chapter 5 provides guidance on preparing family budgets. If your expected income during unemployment is going to be insufficient to meet your expenses, and it probably will be, you can plan how to close the gap. This will involve a combination of reducing your living expenses and finding other sources of income. Chapter 15 provides guidance for those who do lose their jobs.

Reduce Current Spending in Order to Increase Savings

The two best things that you can do to prepare for financial adversity, like job loss, go hand in hand: reduce your current level of spending and increase your savings. Setting aside some savings now may come in very handy in helping you meet your living expenses later if you become unemployed. A financial cushion is the best way to soften the trauma of unemployment. It is bad enough that you may have to go through the job-hunting process. But it would be doubly unfortunate to have to worry about making ends meet at the same time. So take action now to increase or begin a savings program. Chapter 6 provides ideas for putting your expenses on a diet, and Chapter 14 shows ways to get the best interest on money that you may need in a short time.

Manage Your Debt

If you have outstanding loans, such as auto and credit card loans, you may be wondering whether you should reduce them in anticipation of unemployment rather than increase your savings level. In general, if you are concerned about losing your job, you should be careful not to fall behind on your debt payments, but you're better off putting extra money in savings rather than paying extra to reduce your debt. Why? If you do lose your job, you may have to dip into savings to meet living expenses. If you had used the money to reduce your debts, this potential financial cushion would not be available to you. Of course, paying down high-interest debt is a good idea under more normal economic circumstances. Your financial uncertainty, however, requires that you establish a generous emergency fund rather than reduce your indebtedness.

Adjust Your Tax Withholding

If you are quite certain that you are going to be laid off, you might want to arrange to have less income tax withheld from your paycheck (by increasing the number of exemptions) so that your take-home pay is increased. This will provide extra income to put into savings that you can eventually use when you are unemployed. Since your income will almost certainly drop when you are laid off, the taxes owed will probably balance out by the end of the year, even though you decreased your tax withholdings while you were still employed.

Defer Large Expenditures

Now is *not* the time to make any large purchases, such as a new car or home improvements. These commitments should be deferred at least until you are confident that your job is not in jeopardy. Even then, you should be very careful about making major financial commitments when the economy is on the rocks. Many people are tempted to make large expenditures during economic downturns because sellers of these products and services—automobile dealers and home improvement contractors, for example—offer bargain prices to attract customers when business is slow. People who are blessed with abundant cash reserves and reliable future income prospects may take advantage of these offers, but you would be better off deferring all major purchases until your job uncertainty is resolved. Besides, the bargain prices aren't that much lower, believe me.

Plan for Continuity of Insurance Coverage

One of the worst things people can do during a period of financial adversity is to let their insurance coverage lapse. Stories abound of people who thought they couldn't afford to continue their health insurance coverage, only to find their finances wiped out by an uninsured illness. Be sure to include a provision in your budget for paying insurance premiums. Also, decide ahead of time how you are going to replace your employer-provided health and life insurance when it expires. Your company is probably required to allow you to continue your group health coverage for a period of 18 months (or perhaps longer) after termination as long as you pay the premiums. Look into it.

Review Your Investments

If you expect to lose your job, you should review your investments for two reasons. First, you need to assess how much of your invested funds can be readily converted into cash to meet living expenses if the need arises. Second, you may decide to sell some of your low-yield investments, such as stocks that pay little or no dividends. You can reinvest this money in interest-earning securities that will provide you with higher current income to help you meet expenses when your salary is temporarily eliminated. You must weigh the tax effects of any investment transactions, however. For example, it may not make sense to sell very-low-tax-basis stock investments in order to buy interest-earning investments, since the capital gains taxes you will have to pay after the sale will reduce the resources available for reinvestment in interest-earning securities. See Part III of this book for recommendations on investing in uncertain times.

Safe Money Checklist

If You Think You're Going to Lose Your Job

✔ Make a realistic assessment of the possibility that you might lose your job and when you might lose it.

✔ Prepare yourself mentally for a potential job loss so that it will not be devastating if and when it happens. Being prepared may enable you to negotiate a better severance.

✔ Prepare a budget that assumes that you will be laid off and includes a plan of action that balances income and expenses.

✔ Increase your savings rate or begin to save, so that you will have a cushion if you lose your job.

✔ Don't make any large expenditures while your job outlook is uncertain.

✔ Plan now to ensure that you maintain adequate insurance coverage during your period of unemployment.

✔ Make sure that your savings are invested appropriately in light of your uncertain financial future.

17 EVALUATING EARLY-RETIREMENT INCENTIVE PLANS

My company has offered an early-retirement incentive plan to everyone in my department. I wasn't planning to retire for a few more years, but the offer seems attractive. I like my job, but I might get laid off anyway if things get worse. I don't know what to do.

E arly-retirement incentive programs are a common means of achieving a reduction in the workforce, and for companies in the midst of a slowing business climate, downsizing, mergers, or takeovers, they have been one way to reduce layoffs. As business conditions worsen, a growing number of larger employers will be offering early-retirement incentives as a way to reduce the work-force as humanely as possible. The advantages and disadvantages of the plans are very clear cut and quantifiable for employers.

In a recession, early retirement sounds particularly appealing to employees, since times are tough and there are usually no guarantees that they'll be able to keep their jobs if they don't accept the offer. The plans are fairly compelling, but on the other hand, many of these programs offer a lot less than meets the eye. To make matters worse, chances are that if you're con-fronted with an early-retirement incentive plan, you'll have only a limited amount of time to evaluate the offer. You can't be too careful in assessing something that will dramatically affect the rest of your life.

WHAT ARE YOUR REAL CHOICES?

Before trying to compare working and retiring by drawing up a list of the pros and cons, or trying to project your retired versus working income and expenses for the next 30 years, you must assess your situation realistically. Do you really *have* to take the deal offered you, or do you think you still have some choices? What is your likelihood of continued employment if you decline the current offer? You're on the inside now; have you noticed anything that indicates how badly the company is being affected by the recession? If things are really bad, the incentive plan might be only the beginning of a reduction in the workforce, with the result that you will be laid off anyway, have your pay frozen or cut, or be transferred to a less desirable job. You should consider whether there have already been layoffs at the company and, if so, how they were implemented. If you're worried about your job future at the company, the early-retirement plan may well be your most palatable option. If future layoffs appear likely, you may have little choice but to participate in an early-retirement program.

One clue as to what will happen to your job if you try to keep it may be given in the early-retirement offer itself. If it's limited to one plant or one department, it probably signals significant changes for those who remain. If, on the other hand, the company is offering the option across the board, say to all employees over age 55 with more than 10 years' experience, your job may not be subject to future eliminations. In general, the narrower the cut, the worse it bodes for those who refuse it. If you have no choice but to take the early-retirement offer, you must plan for the future. If you have some choice, you still need to plan for the future, and your plans may influence whether or not you will take the offer.

Assuming that you do have a choice and that you still enjoy working, you've got a lot of factors to weigh before making your decision. It's true that many early-retirement incentive programs look appealing at first glance; incentives may include additional or enhanced pension benefits, retiree health insurance, and lump-sum cash benefits. However, you should keep in mind that the high cost of living and the erosion of purchasing power caused by inflation may make such benefits much less attractive in only a few years.

LESS THAN MEETS THE EYE

To put it bluntly, most people cannot afford to retire early—even if they think they can, and even with a generous company-sponsored incentive plan. This is even truer today than it was a couple of years ago, given the implosion of stock prices that has left many retirement savings accounts a mere shadow of what they once were. If you would like to take early retirement, you need to take a hard look at how easily you will be able to meet your living expenses, not just now, but also 10, 20, and 30 years from now. Many employees who leave their jobs under company-sponsored early-retirement plans discover later that they won't have enough income to support themselves very well.

Company-sponsored early-retirement incentive plans often look particularly appealing because the company benefits officer shows you how much more you'll receive with the plan than if you were to quit your job now without it. However, unless you were considering retiring anyway, this isn't really a useful comparison. A better comparison would be between the package that is being offered and what you could expect if you stayed in your job as long as you originally intended. You will be sacrificing something; if you weren't, how would your company be saving money?

For example, even a beefed-up early-retirement pension is likely to be considerably smaller than the pension you could expect if you continued to work. That's because your pension is probably based on the average of what you earned in the last few years you worked. Even if the early-retirement incentive plan adds bonus years of employment and bonus years of age to your pension formula, it won't be able to make up the difference between your average salary for the last five years and your presumably higher average salary for your last five years if you were to continue working. Of course, if it looks as if this economic crisis is going to hurt your company so badly that those hypothetical future pay increases would never materialize, then the difference between retiring now and retiring later shrinks.

If you're ready to quit your job anyway, and the extra years of leisure are worth the reduced benefits, then the crucial issue for you is not how the early-retirement package compares with the normal retirement options, but whether the package is sufficient to meet your retirement income needs. To answer that you will have to project your retirement income and expenses.

Budgeting for Early Retirement

Before accepting or rejecting any early-retirement incentive plan, you must project your income and expenses until age 95 (yes, there's a good chance you'll live that long, if not longer), taking inflation into account. The following guidelines should help you estimate some of those items more accurately. Be honest and realistic. You don't want to run out of money at a time when your prospects of reentering the workforce are slim to nil.

- Many people mistakenly assume that their tax burden will lighten significantly at retirement. You will avoid some taxes, but on the other hand, the new administration is very clear in its plan to raise taxes. While these planned tax hikes are intended to affect only the very rich (Washington's definition of the very rich: anyone who makes more than a member of Congress), given the trillion-dollar budget deficits and ambitious spending programs, even the less rich may see higher taxes.

- Some people may overestimate how much their living expenses will drop. Most retirees spend 65 percent as much as they did while working, to maintain roughly the same lifestyle. Some spend more.
- One commonly overlooked expense is health insurance. Most early-retirement incentive plans extend your company health insurance coverage after you leave work. If yours doesn't, you'll have to pay high premiums for an individually purchased policy until you become eligible for Medicare at 65.
- Many early retirees count on working part-time to supplement their retirement income. Part-time employment answers the two most frequent complaints of early retirees, too much time and too little money, but don't count on this option. Depending on your job experience and your locale, good part-time jobs that are financially and emotionally rewarding may not be as plentiful as you think. Right now, the economic conditions that caused your company to offer you the window incentive are also affecting your potential employers. Good full-time jobs may be even harder to find than part-time jobs. Don't simply assume that you'll be able to get a full- or part-time job. On the other hand, if you can line one up before the early-retirement incentive plan deadline, you may hit a financial home run.

OTHER FACTORS TO CONSIDER

You also must weigh the effects of an early retirement on your other sources of retirement income.

- **Social security benefits.** Your social security benefits will be reduced if you opt to collect before full retirement age, currently age 66 for people born before 1960. Not only are the monthly checks lower, but the future cost of living increases are also proportionally lower because they are calculated from a lower initial benefit amount. As a result, benefits for early retirees will lag further and further behind inflation.

- **Retirement savings.** Any funds that you have in retirement savings plans, annuities, and other investment accounts earmarked to eventually provide retirement income may be affected by your early-retirement incentive plan decision. You will have contributed to these accounts for fewer years when you retire, and you probably will begin withdrawing from the plans sooner than you otherwise would have. Even if you can afford to delay payments and avoid the penalties that may be assessed if you tap into retirement savings plan accounts before age 59½, there will be less available to withdraw than there would have been if you had contributed for a few more years.

One rule of thumb I use in advising people who are considering early retirement is: if your projections show that you will *have* to begin drawing social security benefits at age 62 to help meet living expenses or that you will *have* to start tapping into your retirement savings plans before your mid-sixties, you may not be able to afford to retire early.

THE BRIGHTER SIDE

If you've been looking forward to an early retirement that might be augmented by an early-retirement plan, these caveats may seem discouraging. Early retirement is a very attractive prospect for many people, and the current dismal economy makes daily work life less exciting, if not downright depressing. It *is* possible to retire early and retire well, but you need to be very certain of your long-term financial security. If you have accumulated sufficient personal resources, your projections may show that you can afford an early retirement under the terms offered by your employer. You may want to ask an accountant to help you make your retirement income and expense projections. All I ask is that you be very careful and realistic in projecting your income and expenses until age 95. If the numbers work and if you want to take early retirement, by all means do so.

Safe Money Checklist

Evaluating an Early-Retirement Incentive Plan

✔ Determine how much choice you really have. What will happen to your company in the future? What will happen to your job? If the likely alternative is being fired, take the offer.

✔ If you have a choice, compare the package with the retirement benefits you would receive if you continued to work—not to those you would receive if you retired immediately without the package.

✔ Examine how you feel about your job, and consider how you would like to spend the next 30 or 40 years of your life. Would you enjoy the leisure of leaving your job, or would you feel bored and restless?

✔ Project your retirement income and expenses until age 95. The retirement benefits that look so generous now will look a lot different when you see how 30 or more years of inflation can erode your purchasing power.

✔ Determine how your other retirement resources would be affected by an early retirement.

✔ Ascertain how long your severance pay and personal resources alone would be able to support you so that you can avoid steep penalties on early retirement fund withdrawals and let your personal retirement accounts accumulate tax free.

✔ Examine your prospects for continuing employment realistically. If your company offers postemployment job counseling, take advantage of it.

18 Finding a Job in Tough Times

Whether your financial situation is pretty good or pretty dismal, you need to approach a job search with the same enthusiasm and dedication that you would apply to any new and challenging task. The fact that everything you read about the plight of the unemployed in this job market is downright depressing doesn't mean that your prospects are bleak. Sure, you'll be discouraged by the rejections, but you *will* succeed sooner rather than later as long as you sustain your effort. Rather than focusing on the bad news, think about the tales of multimillionaires who started out unemployed. Economic contractions routinely breed opportunities. Old companies that failed to work are replaced with new ideas and new energy. You'll feel better if you look at those possibilities rather than at the negative factors that may have led to your need for work. (See Chapter 15 if you have just lost your job. Chapter 16 provides guidance if you think you may lose your job.)

YOUR JOB SEARCH

Your first job search task should be to determine where the job opportunities lie. In the United States, for example, jobs are growing in the fields of health care and energy, to name just two.

Get organized and mobilized. Examine your income, expenses, savings, and investments. (See Chapters 5 and 6 for help on making ends meet.) Determine whether you qualify for placement assistance or job retraining. Apply immediately if you qualify for government benefits like unemployment insurance. If your spouse or partner is working, that should help.

Set up a daily action plan and stick to it. Consider taking these steps:

- Target companies that you feel could use your services and might hire you. Do Internet searches for job banks. Many government unemployment offices have links to state, private-sector, federal, veterans, and military transition job banks, as well as résumé and interview services. Other sources include www.Monster.com, www.CareerBuilder.com, and www.HotJobs.com.
- Be alert for jobs in industries that may soon be growing, such as infrastructure and alternative energy, homeland security, the defense industry, and research industries that are experiencing job shortages. www.CareerBuilder.com has quarterly job forecasts. Check the Bureau of Labor

Statistics (www.bls.gov) for information about areas of job growth.

- Network by renewing contacts with colleagues, old friends, and people with whom you've done business in the past. Talk to neighbors and relatives. Don't be afraid to call people you haven't spoken with in years, especially if you had a good relationship with them in the past. Attend outside meetings and conferences. Get in touch with professional organizations in your area and nationwide. Read local business publications.
- Take a part-time job or consider freelancing to keep extra money coming in. You also can make new contacts this way. When the economy turns around, you might be offered a full-time position. Check out www.MyPartTimePRO.com for a list of part-time regular or professional jobs. Don't forget eBay! Consider turning hobbies into businesses.
- If necessary, seek professional advice on setting up a résumé, writing cover letters, and interview skills. Contact a job recruiter in your area.
- Network online and create a positive Internet personality at job sites like Monster.com, as well as network sites such as www.facebook.com, www.linkedin.com, and www.Ning.com. Create a virtual résumé in addition to a hard copy one.
- Contact employers directly at Web sites like www.Flipdog.com and DirectEmployers.com.
- Keep a level head. Remember that you always have choices. Don't feel as if you are cornered.
- Temporary employment agencies might help keep the money coming in.

- If you've tried all these tactics to no avail, there are a couple of other options that may bear fruit. First, consider doing volunteer work. This should prop up your spirits and keep you busy between job interviews. Also, a volunteer job can account on your résumé for the period of your unemployment, and employers may be impressed by your resourcefulness during a time when far too many unemployed people sit at home feeling sorry for themselves. Another option to consider is whether additional education and/or training might improve your opportunities. Analyze what low-cost training options might beef up your skills or prepare you for a promising new career.

HELPING YOUR CHILD FIND PART-TIME WORK

Another unfortunate by-product of a weak employment market is that it's likely to be tough for high school and college-age children to find summer jobs and part-time school year jobs. Local, state, and federal grants to nonprofits that provide summer jobs to students are being slashed. Plus, many adults who are out of work are taking jobs at fast-food restaurants and retail stores, leaving fewer opportunities for teenagers.

- The key is to get your children psyched up. Today's economic environment can teach them helpful lessons about courage and perseverance. They will become particularly strong and resistant to life's hard knocks if they can learn at a young age how to bounce back from rejection.

- Like out-of-work adults, teenagers and young adults need a game plan. They should have a well-written résumé and cover letter ready to show employers.
- Kids can go to www.Myfirstpaycheck.com for a free résumé.
- To get a summer job in this competitive marketplace, young adults must be persistent and polite. They need to dress well and make eye contact with interviewers to make a good first impression. Plus, they should follow up with a thank-you after each interview.
- They should check for jobs around administrative offices at school. Parents and kids should also network with friends, relatives, and neighbors.
- Even if they are unsuccessful, a little creativity can help. Cutting lawns, delivering newspapers, babysitting, and running errands for senior citizens are always great ways to make some money. Consider that billionaire investor Warren Buffett started his career by selling chewing gum. Then, he saved up his profits.

Safe Money Checklist

Finding a Job in Tough Times

✔ Approach your job search with enthusiasm and dedication; make it a full-time job.

✔ If jobs in your field are scarce, consider applying in job sectors that are growing.

✔ Cast a wide net, including contacting current and past colleagues and using the Internet to identify job openings.

✔ If necessary, use professionals to help you polish your résumé and enhance your interview skills.

✔ Seek part-time work or volunteer work as a way to fill gaps in your resume, demonstrate initiative, and feel better about yourself.

✔ Above all, don't get discouraged by rejection. By focusing on the task at hand, you'll succeed in your job search.

✔ The recession means fewer summer and part-time jobs for students. You can provide important life-long lessons by encouraging your child to be creative in the job search and urging him or her to bounce back from rejection.

19 COPING WITH DEBT PROBLEMS

Every day I'm getting calls from insistent creditors and collection agencies. I'm trying to pay my bills. Don't they realize times are tough?

It is very easy to fall into debt problems, and not just from over-spending and overborrowing. When the economy weakens, individuals and families who were coping with their loans in good times now find themselves having trouble meeting their obligations. The current credit crisis is like none other that we have experienced.

- Millions of workers are jobless.
- Incomes are stagnant.
- The worldwide stock markets have plummeted.

- Strapped lenders are tightening loan requirements, if they're lending at all.
- Many lenders are in such dire financial straits that they've stepped up collection efforts.

If you find that you're experiencing problems paying your bills or if you anticipate that this may be the case in the near future, you may be able to take steps to keep anxious creditors at bay, get your debts under control, and prevent overdue bills from having too adverse an effect on your life, or even on your credit rating.

WORKING WITH YOUR CREDITORS

The first warning sign of overindebtedness is late payments. Late payments result in late charges, which can be substantial and can affect your credit record. If you will not be able to meet any loan payment, including your credit cards, act *before* the actual delinquency occurs, if at all possible. Explain the circumstances to the creditor. If you contact it before *it* is compelled to contact you, it will be much more likely to believe that you intend to pay off the debt, and it is much more likely that you will be able to agree on a more convenient payment date, more favorable loan terms, a temporary reduction in payments, or a waiver of late charges. Do not avoid calls or letters from creditors under any circumstances. Your creditors would much rather know that you are trying to work things out than fear that you are trying to evade the whole debt. Most creditors prefer working with you than repossessing the goods or taking you to court, which is time-consuming and costs them more in the long run. But keeping creditors at bay is possible only if you are honestly trying to get your financial life in order. You must commit to working out your problems.

- Reduce your living expenses. Chapter 6 may help.
- Work out a plan first to keep current on your loans and then to pay them down. This means that you'll have to go without some of the luxuries that may be the cause of your problems in the first place.
- Prioritize your loans so that nothing important is jeopardized. If you can only afford to make the minimum payment on your credit card loan because the mortgage is due, don't miss the mortgage payment. On the other hand, if you ever have a little extra cash to spare, work down the high-interest credit card debt before paying extra against lower-interest, but more important debts.
- If your credit problems are particularly acute, unload some possessions; for example, sell your car.
- Restructure your debt. Discuss payment options with your creditors or credit counselor. Once new terms have been agreed to, it is crucial that you abide by them.
- Whatever the situation, keep the lines of communication open with your creditors.
- Cut up all but one of your credit cards.

As with many problems in life, the deeper into debt you get, the harder it is to get out. Also, the deeper into debt you get, the more vulnerable you are to any number of schemes designed to rob you of your money just when you need it the most. If you have credit problems, talk to your creditors or a legitimate credit counseling service. Do not be tempted to fall for offers from loan sharks, who charge illegally high interest rates, or loan consolidation schemes, unless they are offered by a legitimate bank or other well-known financial institution. There are a lot of infomercials that also prey on those with debt problems. They can all be summed up in one word: bogus.

NEXT, TRY CREDIT COUNSELING

If you have financial problems that you can't resolve on your own, the next step is to consult a credit counselor. Various institutions offer such counseling, including many banks and credit unions, family service agencies, and nonprofit consumer credit counseling organizations. If you are slightly overextended, the agency will usually help you develop a repayment plan for a nominal monthly fee. The agency may take monthly payments from you and distribute them to your creditors. The agency also talks to the creditors and may get them to agree to delayed or reduced payments. By the way, make sure that you are dealing with a credit counselor who is affiliated with a legitimate *nonprofit* consumer credit counseling service. There are a number of charlatans out there who hold themselves out as nonprofit credit counselors and who have slick TV advertising campaigns, but who will do nothing more than wreak further havoc on your financial situation. Contact the following organization to find a worthy credit counselor:

> National foundation for Credit Counseling
> (www.nfcc.org)

One important thing to remember: if you use a consumer credit counseling organization, it will be reported to the credit bureaus and noted on your credit record. That fact should not deter you from using a credit counseling service, particularly if your only other alternative is filing for bankruptcy. While you may ultimately have to resort to bankruptcy, give credit counseling a try first. Chapter 28 provides some guidance on filing for bankruptcy, which, by the way, is not the end of the world.

Safe Money Checklist

If You Are Having Problems Handling Your Debts

- ✔ Contact your creditors before they contact you.
- ✔ Work out a reasonable payment plan that your creditors agree to and that you can stick to.
- ✔ Reduce your living expenses so that you can devote more funds to getting current and reducing your debt.
- ✔ Prioritize your bills, so that you don't jeopardize important possessions.
- ✔ Pay off higher-interest bills first.
- ✔ Keep only one credit card.
- ✔ Stay away from loan consolidations if you possibly can.
- ✔ If necessary, seek help from a legitimate consumer credit counseling organization.

20 ADVICE FOR HOMEOWNERS

Housing prices are declining in our neighborhood, and there have even been a couple of foreclosures. Maybe we should never have bought the house. We're having some trouble making our mortgage payments every month, and we're not sure what to do.

H ousing prices have been declining in most parts of the country, fueling the fear that the national housing recession will worsen and then recover very slowly. Millions of homeowners are "underwater" in their mortgage, which means that they owe more on the house than it is currently worth. If that describes your situation, you're far from alone. In many locales around the country, more than 40 percent of mortgaged homes are underwater. If you're worried about what will happen to your home, remember that there's really no such thing as a national housing market and no way to make generalizations that include everyone. Like any other worthwhile investment, real estate periodically declines in value. In the past, real estate downturns have turned out to be just temporary interruptions in the long-term rise in home values. There's no reason to believe that the current housing downturn will be any different.

A HOME IS STILL A GOOD INVESTMENT

Homeownership *is* all it's cracked up to be. It gives you tax advantages, control over housing costs, and the security and pride of ownership. While you own your home, it gives you those benefits, whether or not it's appreciating in price at the moment. Appreciation can be a great advantage of owning a home, but it is not the only or most important advantage.

A home is a wonderful investment, but it is not a short-term one, so don't get depressed by short-term price fluctuations. Over the long run, housing prices normally beat inflation, so when your house declines in value temporarily, don't panic. Unless you need to sell or borrow against the value of your home, changes in its paper value don't mean much.

COPING WITH THE CURRENT HOME AND MORTGAGE SITUATION

Here are some suggestions if you're among the millions of home-owners who were blindsided by problems in both the real estate and mortgage markets. If you've locked into a low, fixed-rate mortgage and you have no intention of moving, you have little to worry about. Just be patient until the market turns around. However, if you've signed on to a mortgage with an adjustable rate that's apt to rise, particularly if you expect your monthly payment to double or quadruple, now's the time to act.

If Your Credit Is in Good Standing

If you're keeping current on all your loans, but you fear that your mortgage rate or payment could skyrocket, there are a couple of relatively painless options available to you.

- **Refinancing.** First, see if your existing lender will convert your adjustable-rate mortgage to a fixed-rate mortgage that you can better afford over the long term. By trying your current lender first, you may be able to save on closing costs and up-front fees. If that doesn't work, shop around. Don't rule out savings institutions or credit unions. However, before you hand over any money to any lender for a new loan, first get your lender's opinion on whether your appraisal is likely to qualify you for the amount you aim to borrow. If it's unlikely, forget it. Your deal may not go through, and you certainly don't want to waste your money on an appraisal fee. On the other hand, if you are likely to qualify for a loan large enough to pay off your existing loan, seek the lowest rate and fees possible. If possible, avoid extending the term, a move that can add to your debt. Try not to have finance charges rolled into your loan. While it might seem like an attractive option to shorten your 25- to 30-year term to, say, 15 years at a lower interest rate, expect to make larger monthly payments if you do this. By contrast, with the longer-term loan, you still can make extra monthly payments to reduce the principal provided that you have no prepayment penalty. Yet you retain the option to make smaller payments if the need arises. This can come in handy if you become financially squeezed.

- **Selling your home.** First determine your home's true value. Obtain a comparative market analysis from a real estate agent. Or, consider calling in a few real estate agents for an opinion (see Chapter 21). You want to know that you'll be able to get enough money for your home to pay off the amount you owe.

If You're Having Financial Problems

Answer these questions:

- Is it getting tough to pay your credit card debt?
- Are you using your credit cards for everyday expenses, like groceries?
- Are you having trouble paying your monthly bills?

If you've answered yes to any of these questions, your problem with meeting your mortgage payments may be more serious. You'll need to act quickly. However, resist the fastest fixes. Most of them are scams in which con artists trick those who are most desperate to sign over the deed to their homes. Once the deed is transferred, it's sayonara! Meanwhile, you still owe the mortgage. Be skeptical of offers to

- Pay your mortgage and rent your home back to you.
- Sign over a partial interest in your home to one or more persons to halt foreclosure proceedings. Each holder may file for bankruptcy, resulting in a stay being issued by the bankruptcy court. While this may temporarily stop foreclosure proceedings, there's a good chance that the scam artist is not paying your mortgage, as promised. Meanwhile, you'll still owe your mortgage and the accompanying fees.
- Refinance your loan. Many such offers trick you into signing documents that you think are for a new loan. However, the signed documents transfer the deed to your property.

A more viable option is to seek free or low-cost counseling from a counselor approved by the U.S. Department of Housing and Urban Development. Call (800) 569-4287. The counseling agency can help guide you to more realistic solutions.

Do you feel that you're in trouble because you've been tricked into paying unusually high fees or an unfairly high interest rate? In that case, it could pay to consult with an attorney. Courts increasingly are ruling against lenders in challenges involving abusive or "predatory" loans. A court win not only might cut the amount you owe, but could cover your legal fees. You can search for a consumer attorney who might take your case — perhaps on a contingency-fee basis — at www.naca.net.

If You Want to Remain
in Your Home

Prefer to remain in your home? In that case a loan modification may be an attractive option. Ask your lender for its loan mitigation department. You might be able to negotiate a temporary suspension of payments or lower payments in exchange for a term extension. It's possible that your lender may even agree to forgive some of your debt. Sometimes, such a deal may require you to give up a percentage of your home's appreciation when you sell. But before you seek debt forgiveness, round up your mortgage paperwork and calculate your own income and expenses. You'll need to figure out exactly how much you can afford to pay each month. Then, you'll have to sell your lender on the best possible deal for yourself. Your objective should be to avoid increasing your debt through added interest charges or by extending the term of your loan. Keep in mind that a loan modification probably will appear on your credit report. It never hurts, though, to ask your lender not to report it. An interest-rate adjustment is not reported to the credit bureaus or factored into your credit score. So it never hurts to ask your lender for an interest-rate reduction. Also, if you're in the military or you're a disaster victim, you might be entitled to some specific relief.

Meanwhile, there's some good news if you can get your lender to forgive debt on your principal residence. You no longer need to pay federal income tax on that forgiven amount—at least for 2007, 2008, and 2009. However, this new rule, under the Mortgage Forgiveness Debt Relief Act of 2007, does not apply to second homes.

IF YOU WANT OUT OF YOUR HOME

If you'd like to sell, but you owe more than the house is worth (you're underwater), you may be able to convince your lender to agree to a "short sale." This means that the lender accepts payment of less than the full amount you owe. Make sure you fiercely negotiate this deal if you can, read your contract with a fine-tooth comb (ideally, ask a lawyer to review it), and watch for extra fees and commissions.

You may also offer your lender the deed in lieu of foreclosure. With this arrangement, you voluntarily transfer your deed to your lender. This probably won't work, however, if you already have other liens on your home.

The principal advantage of this arrangement is that it immediately releases you from most or all of the personal indebtedness associated with the mortgage loan. You also avoid the public notoriety of a foreclosure proceeding. However, it's always important to speak with an attorney about this and other ways to get out from under your mortgage.

FORECLOSURE

If you feel overwhelmed by your situation and you have exhausted the alternatives described here, you may need to consider foreclosure. As with any credit trouble, contact the lender as soon as you anticipate a problem (see Chapter 19). Lenders and the government are continually implementing programs to help homeowners avert foreclosure, so keep up to date on any available programs. They don't do this out of the kindness of their hearts; foreclosure is a long and expensive process, during which they don't get any payments. Besides, by the time they assume control of the property, lenders often wind up losing a substantial portion of the original mortgage on a foreclosure.

Lenders would much rather work out some way to avoid foreclosing. A "workout" is a plan to resolve the situation. A workout probably will not lower the amount you owe (although some plans being considered by both the government and lenders may reduce the amount owed), but it might change your payment schedule so that you can make lower payments now and make up for them later. Other workout arrangements include changing from an adjustable-rate to a fixed-rate mortgage or extending the length of the loan so that you can make up for missed payments. If you can't agree on a workout, some lenders and mortgage insurance companies will help you sell your home—even if it won't bring in enough to pay them off (a short sale, as described previously). If you owe the bank more money than the sale raises, and you absolutely can't pay the balance, the bank may grant you an interest-free loan. Obviously, the bank doesn't want to do that, but it usually still loses less that way than in a foreclosure.

Banks generally lose in a foreclosure, but what about you? Houses are losing value so fast in many areas that homeowners find that they owe the bank more than the house is now worth! But the mortgage you signed is a legal document that binds you to pay the debt no matter what. A foreclosure remains on your credit record for seven years. It can make it very difficult to get credit, and it can also impair the credit you already have. In addition, there's no guarantee that the bank can get back the value of the mortgage when it sells your house. If you don't repay it the difference, the lender may be able to take your other assets and perhaps part of your wages for many years to make up the shortfall. Not all states allow such "deficiency judgments," however.

If you, like so many other families, lose your home to foreclosure as a result of the Great Recession, it's not the end of the world. It will take you time to rebuild your credit, but stories abound of families who were able to qualify for a mortgage within just a few years of a foreclosure.

DEALING WITH CREDIT LINE REDUCTIONS

The real estate recession has led to another problem. Because of declining home values, lenders have been freezing home equity credit lines and/or slashing their credit limits—even to their most creditworthy customers. The reason: home values have dropped, and lenders fear that in the event of a default, they will be unable to recoup their losses. In addition, the credit crunch has motivated lenders to terminate the credit cards of borrowers who have not used them and slash credit card limits for cardholders whom they consider to be greater risks.

If you're already having problems meeting your monthly obligations, these moves can exacerbate your problems. A canceled credit card or lower credit line can lower your credit score. This, in turn, can trigger higher interest rates on other loans or eliminate your ability to borrow altogether—just when you may need more money. Do you think that your credit line may soon be frozen because of a decline in property value and that you may need cash? In that case, you might consider drawing down the credit line and putting the cash in a safe place, like bank CDs and savings accounts.

Safe Money Checklist

Tips for Homeowners during Tough Times

✔ If you don't need to sell, don't worry about your paper losses. Your home provides you with a lot more than appreciation in value, and if you can ride out this recession, it will provide you with that, too.

✔ Try to refinance into a fixed-rate mortgage if you're saddled with an adjustable-rate mortgage with payments that have risen or might rise considerably.

✔ If you are having or anticipate having trouble making your mortgage payments, talk to the lender about ways to avoid losing your home. The lender can help only if you ask, and you may find that the lender or the government has a program that will let you keep your home.

✔ Prepare in advance for the possibility that lenders may curtail your home equity line of credit or credit card limits.

21 ADVICE FOR HOME SELLERS

If you can avoid selling your home in a weak market, you probably should, but if your circumstances change and you want or have to sell now, or if you've really wanted to trade up and you think this is a great time to do so, here are some tips for making the sale as painless and as profitable as possible.

SELLING IN A SOFT MARKET

Set a Realistic Asking Price

Have you wondered why, in the midst of the worst real estate market in decades, some homes in your neighborhood sell in a few weeks, while others stay on the market for years? The difference is the price the owner thinks the place is worth. If other home prices in your neighborhood have come down, yours has too. Don't delude yourself into thinking that your home is the only one within 1,000 miles that hasn't declined in value over the past couple of years.

It doesn't make sense to list the house at more than it's currently worth. You won't get your price, and it'll be harder to interest brokers when you finally lower the price. Besides, buyers who notice how long the house has been on the market may wonder what's keeping it from selling and stay away from it. The ideal sales price will be one that is a bit lower than comparable properties in your locale, but that still has some wiggle room for negotiation, because prospective buyers know full well that people aren't lined up at your home with full-price offers.

Use a Real Estate Agent

While it may be tempting to try to sell the house yourself without the help of a real estate agent, a slow market is precisely the time you need the expertise of an experienced real estate agent. Find one of the best agents in town, and she will be eager to help you sell your manse. Whenever the housing market is undergoing a recession, the real estate agents are suffering a depression. Your agent will be very motivated to orchestrate a sale. She will deal directly with potential buyers, so you won't have to take calls or endure visits from some doofus who just graduated from a "How to Buy Real Estate for No Money Down" course.

Make Your House Stand Out

Increase the appeal of the home by making sensible, modestly priced upgrades. Painting, new carpets, and some front yard landscaping can go a long way in attracting buyers. On the other hand, avoid making major improvements, as they probably will not sway a potential buyer in a weak market. With a little effort, you can make your house a little more memorable to prospective buyers who are tired from a long day of traipsing through open houses. Clean up the whole house, even inside the closets and other storage spaces, to make it look bigger and more appealing. Keep the lawn mowed, and clean up around the front door in case the prospective buyers are standing there for a while. (Do you remember how many times you drove by your house before you bought it?) Put on a colorful bedspread or throw a rug by the fireplace. Obviously, the new owners won't be buying your furniture, but it will affect the way they see the house.

Don't Buy a New House before Selling the Old One

Unless you've got truckloads of ready cash, buying a new home before selling the old one can be a big mistake. This is true even in strong markets, and doubly so when markets are weak. There's nothing more depressing than moving into a new home, with all the associated expenses, while still maintaining that old albatross. Moreover, it's usually tougher to sell an empty home. If you want to buy a new house while prices are low and you don't mind being a temporary landlord, you might consider renting your current one instead of selling it right away, but only if you can afford to buy the new home without selling the old one. The rental income will help you carry the costs of two homes, and you can wait until housing prices improve to sell the old one.

Tips for Facilitating the Sale

- Alleviate as many concerns that a buyer might have as possible before putting the house on the market. The home inspection is one concern, so consider having your home inspected by a certified home inspector. While the buyer will certainly have another inspector look at the property, a relatively clean inspection report may persuade the buyer to make an offer. Also, if you are willing to finance the down payment, make that clear at the outset.
- One of the biggest advantages you can have (as both a home buyer and a home seller) is time. Unless you absolutely have to unload the home as soon as possible, you should expect that making the sale will take time, and that your patience will eventually be rewarded. Patience means that you won't feel compelled to take the first offer that comes along. A patient seller will be less inclined to take the home off the market when there is scant interest in the property. Unless your frustration level is too high, there is no reason to take the house off the market, only to have to go through the listing process anew later on.

Negotiating the Sale

Common wisdom suggests that when you are selling a home during a weak real estate market, you should accept the first offer that comes along. That's most certainly not the case. True, the prospective buyer may be in the driver's seat, but it's still your "car" that the buyer wants to own. If you don't like the offer, you are free to reject it. Again, an experienced real estate agent can be indispensable during stressful negotiations and in advising you along the way. Then, when a deal is struck, you can have more confidence that you got the right price under the circumstances.

Finally, if you're experiencing serious financial problems and need some guidance on ways to keep your home or to get out from under a house that you cannot sell, see Chapter 20.

Safe Money Checklist

Selling a Home in a Buyer's Market

✔ The key to a timely sale is setting a realistic selling price.

✔ Small investments of time and money can make your home more appealing.

✔ Don't buy a new home before selling the old one.

✔ Alleviate as many potential buyers' concerns as possible before listing the home.

✔ A real estate agent can be especially helpful in selling a home in a weak market.

✔ Don't fear rejecting an offer that is substantially below what the house is worth.

22 OPPORTUNITIES FOR HOME BUYERS

We've been saving for a home for ages, but now we're not sure if we should buy. The economy is too messed up, mortgage rates are higher than they were last year, and everyone says that home prices will keep going down. Maybe we'd be better off keeping our money in the bank.

It's scary to think about making any major purchase and taking on a big financial commitment when the economy stinks—and there's no bigger purchase than a home. What happens if you lose your job and can't meet the mortgage payments? How will you feel if you buy a house, but home prices sink after you move in?

Nobody can answer those questions for you, but nobody could in a boom market either. Boom market or recession, you still have to save for the down payment, become familiar with the local real estate market, and put your overall finances in good order so that you can qualify for a mortgage. Thanks to the severity of the sub-prime mortgage crisis, it's even tougher than usual to qualify for a mortgage. If you're afraid that you might need the money you've saved for a house in case you lose your job or undergo other financial duress during the recession, or if you're afraid to commit to 30 years of monthly mortgage payments, then perhaps now is not the time to buy. But if you have saved enough for a down payment and the rest of your finances are relatively well braced for any continuation of difficult economic times (see Chapters 3 and 4), now may be the perfect time to take advantage of a depressed housing market. True, interest rates may be coming down, and housing prices might come down even further. Don't wait around for those things to happen, however. People who wait for ideal conditions usually remain renters. It's not worth worrying about timing the exact moment to take the plunge. Prices are already depressed, and if interest rates drop significantly, you can always refinance your mortgage.

WHY BUY NOW?

Buying a home is one of the best things you can do to achieve financial independence. For most people, the advantages of owning far outweigh the disadvantages. This isn't necessarily a bad time to be buying a home. In fact, it's almost certainly a great time to buy. The Great Recession has caused steep declines in housing prices in almost every area of the country, creating a buyer's market. If you have the money to make a down payment, and you're reasonably sure that your income won't be hurt too much by the recession, now could be the best time to buy in decades.

As times get tougher, plenty of sellers are willing to negotiate. While you may be tempted to buy a home directly from a seller, if this is your first home purchase, you're probably better off working with a real estate agent. Given the dearth of buyers in a weak real estate market, real estate agents are in the midst of their own recessions, so your agent will be particularly diligent in working with you to find the right home. You may also be able to take advantage of some unusual situations, which are described next.

BUYING DISTRESSED REAL ESTATE

Weak local real estate conditions, abetted by infomercials promising great riches from buying distressed real estate, often motivate inexperienced real estate investors to consider buying a distressed property. While there may be an opportunity to pick up a home or other real estate parcel at a bargain price, the pitfalls of attempting to do so are many. Those who complete these transactions successfully are most often specialists, not the average home buyer with grandiose ideas. The following suggestions will help if you become interested in buying distressed real estate.

Unless you can identify a distressed seller early on, most distressed properties end up in one of these three categories:

1. **Foreclosure properties.** A foreclosure property is a home that is in foreclosure, i.e., a notice of default has been filed in the public records, usually because the owner is behind in making mortgage payments. Unless the payments are brought up to date, the lender will take over the property and attempt to sell it at auction.

2. **Short sales.** A short sale generally occurs when a homeowner is in foreclosure, but before the property goes to public auction. The distressed owner attempts to sell the property for less than the amount that is owed on it. However, the lender must agree to the sale.

3. **REOs.** REO is an abbreviation for "real estate owned" by the lending institution. Buying a REO is similar to a short sale, except that the lender has already taken back the property after an unsuccessful foreclosure auction. REO homes are often considered the best way to buy distressed property because the seller is already out of the picture.

Property Condition

If you are considering purchase of a distressed property, you need to be concerned about the condition of the property, particularly if it is still occupied. Many homes may not be available for inspection, leaving the buyer unable to calculate how much it might cost to improve the structure or bring it up to habitable standards. Stories abound of occupants retaliating by trashing the home and removing anything of any value.

If a foreclosure property is occupied, the successful bidder is usually responsible for removing the occupants. You may have second thoughts about buying a distressed property if you have to evict occupants who are already under duress.

Perhaps the most important consideration in buying a distressed property is whether it is indeed a good buy. If the neighborhood in which the property is located is rife with foreclosures, the neighborhood could fall into disrepair, causing home prices to decline further.

If you are interested in considering distressed real estate, use the services of a real estate agent and a real estate attorney who are experienced in these matters.

If you're interested in buying distressed real estate for investment purposes, don't fall for the real estate infomercials. It is extremely difficult to buy properties with little or no money down. Once you own the property, you probably will not be able to receive enough rent to cover your costs. Finally, are you really that anxious to be a landlord?

FINANCING YOUR NEW HOME

If your job is secure, and if you're pretty sure you can make your mortgage payments even if you don't get a raise, then qualifying for a mortgage shouldn't be too difficult. Credit is tighter and lenders are getting stricter, so don't be surprised if they make you produce reams of paperwork prior to granting the mortgage. But on the other hand, fewer people will be applying, and fewer of them will have your qualifications. If you try diligently, and you have been disciplined in your personal financial planning, you will get the mortgage.

What kind of mortgage should you get? *Adjustable-rate mortgage (ARM)* rates are often particularly attractive during a recession because they're normally tied to yields on short-term securities, and given the implosion in stock prices, investors have piled money into short-term securities, driving down interest rates. Just be careful of the provisions for future rate increases in an ARM. Don't take an ARM that has the potential for a huge future interest-rate increase. This is what got the subprime mortgage holders into a pickle.

On the other hand, *fixed-rate mortgages* are attractive if you can lock in a fairly low interest rate. If you can get a fixed-rate mortgage at less than 6 percent, take it. Otherwise, stick with an ARM. You can always refinance into a fixed-rate mortgage later on. It may also be a bit easier to qualify for an ARM.

You may be able to qualify for state programs that facilitate home-ownership for low- and moderate-income families by providing mortgage assistance. These programs vary considerably from state to state, so check to see what's available in your state. In spite of increased fiscal pressures on the states, most of these programs are still being offered. Don't assume that you have too much income to qualify. You may be surprised to find that you do qualify.

Do You Want to Trade Up?

If you're already a homeowner, but you would like to take advantage of cheaper home prices to move or trade up to a costlier manse, be careful. This could turn out to be a good move, but it could also end up being a major-league financial headache. Here are some suggestions:

- Don't assume that your home hasn't lost value during the real estate slump. It has, so don't delude yourself into thinking that you'll get top dollar for your home and pay bottom dollar for the home you're buying.
- It has always been prudent to sell your home before buying the next one. In a weak economy, this is essential. The last thing you want to do is to carry two homes during such uncertain times. Even if you're loaded with dough, it's a waste of your money.
- If you find the ideal home, but you haven't yet sold yours, the seller may be desperate enough to grant you a contingency that allows you a few months to sell your current home. If you don't sell it, you can rescind the purchase and sale agreement.

Safe Money Checklist

Opportunities for First-Time Home Buyers

✔ If your job and your financial prospects are secure, this could be a great time to buy a home.

✔ During a recession, you may be able to buy a home at a good price through foreclosures and other special circumstances, but you should seek professional help to learn the procedures and the pitfalls.

✔ Even moderate-income people may find that they're
eligible for state programs that facilitate
homeownership.

✔ Home mortgages are available in spite of a tight credit
market.

✔ Consider a fixed-rate mortgage if you can lock in a rate
of less than 6 percent; otherwise, opt for an adjustable-
rate mortgage.

✔ If you want to trade up to another home, sell your
current home before buying the new one.

23 GETTING THE KIDS THROUGH COLLEGE

*We always promised our children that if they studied
hard, they could go to college wherever they wanted. We
were going to take out a home equity loan to help pay
tuition, but housing prices have declined to the point that
our equity is pretty much gone. To make matters worse,
my husband just lost his job. We've got one in college. I'm
afraid we can't afford to keep our promise. Tuition is so
expensive. Don't colleges know there's a recession?*

It has *never* been easy to get children through college, but for
many parents, it's getting even harder for a number of reasons.

• Tuition costs have consistently outpaced inflation
for several decades, but in more prosperous times,

most parents could expect their income at least to keep pace with inflation. During a recession, costs will continue to rise, and college costs will definitely continue to rise even faster, but parents can no longer assume that their income will keep pace. Right now, tuition costs are rising at a 6 percent annual rate. Most parents' incomes aren't.

- Although tuition costs are always too steep for most parents, when the economy is in good shape, government agencies, private organizations, and lenders are ready to help out. The schools themselves have more money to distribute and fewer students who need it. Now, however, federal and state cutbacks have reduced the amount and availability of financial aid. Private aid programs are flooded with applicants, and colleges and universities need more and more of their available funds to meet the needs of enrolled students, decreasing the amount available to new applicants.

- The crisis in the financial markets is also affecting education lenders. While federal loans will continue to be secure, the private lenders are having problems. While the recession will not affect existing loans, future loans are likely to require more stringent approval terms and bear higher interest rates.

That's the bad news. The good news is that the colleges are recognizing that students and their families may be going through some tough financial times. In fact, many colleges are contacting the families of all enrolled students and offering them a range of assistance to make sure that they don't have to drop out for financial reasons.

WHAT TO DO IF YOUR SITUATION WORSENS

Colleges and universities abide by the government's assessment of your financial situation as indicated on the Free Application for Federal Student Aid (FAFSA) form. This assessment is based primarily on your tax return and other information you give about your financial situation over the last year. However, in difficult times, it isn't uncommon for a parent's situation to worsen suddenly and render the agreed-upon level of aid inadequate or the agreed-upon parental contribution unattainable.

Many families count on borrowing against their home or selling investments to meet college costs in a crunch if their circumstances are temporarily impaired. However, turmoil in the economy may foil their good intentions for three reasons.

1. The real estate market has worsened throughout the country, and investment values have declined so much that many parents' assets aren't worth what they once were.
2. Many parents' circumstances have changed to such an extent that they can't qualify for a loan.
3. Parents who were willing to refinance their houses in an emergency are now confronted with severely depressed values and tighter lending standards.

If your financial situation deteriorates, and you've got a kid (or, like me, kids) in college, by all means reapply for financial aid. That means filling out another FAFSA form. While a decline in the value of your home will probably not improve your chances of obtaining financial aid, a big decline in your investments could, perversely, work to your advantage. Also, a loss or reduction in job income will be taken into consideration.

Armed with this information, ask for a review by the college's financial aid office.

Financial aid offices are already facing a large number of such crises. Many of them report a doubling of financial aid requests over the prior year. They assure me that although times are tough, there is assistance available to parents facing difficult financial situations. Clearly, this is a bit of good news for students whose parents have been hit particularly hard.

Here are some alternatives that may be available to help you make up for any unexpected shortfall in meeting college costs:

- A variety of loan programs are available, including Perkins loans, Stafford student loans, and PLUS loans. (Visit www.collegeanswer.com.)
- Most colleges offer emergency loans to students. While these loans may be modest, typically $1,000 or less, they can provide some immediate assistance.
- Colleges will usually revisit financial aid in the middle of a school year if there has been a change in the family's financial status, particularly if a breadwinner has become unemployed.
- While tapping into retirement accounts to pay college costs should be considered only under the most exigent circumstances, money withdrawn by parents who are under age 59½ to pay college costs will usually escape the onerous 10 percent penalty assessed on money taken out before age 59½, although income taxes will be due.

The Strategy

Students should use small supplemental loans offered by the college as a stopgap measure and reapply for financial aid as soon as they can, as they will presumably qualify for more aid. Financial aid offices nationwide stand ready to help you through your tough times. You should consult with them as quickly, honestly, and specifically as you can. They are on your side.

ADVICE FOR THE COLLEGE BOUND

The slumping economy will require parents and students to plan more carefully on ways to meet college costs. Here are some suggestions to close the gap between college costs and family resources.

- Don't delay. Begin planning early.
- Consider lower-cost state schools and private colleges with strong financial aid packages. Some students opt to attend a community college for two years before going to a more expensive four-year college.
- Don't automatically assume that you won't qualify for financial aid. There is no downside to completing the FAFSA forms, and you may be pleasantly surprised. Also, the key to getting more financial aid is often simply asking for it.
- Research scholarships. Some resourceful families cobble together several small scholarships that amount to a few thousand dollars each year.
- Speak to college financial aid officers in advance of making a decision. If they really want the student to attend, the college may be able to sweeten the package.

Take the Guesswork Out of 529 Plans

State-sponsored 529 plans are the best way to save for college, but you have to be careful how the money is invested, particularly as your children approach college age. The best way to protect the money along the way is to choose the "age-based" 529 plan investment alternative, which is offered by all 529 plans. The age-based option will automatically but gradually change the investment mix as the pupil nears college age. The younger the child is, the higher the percentage of the money in the plan that will be invested in stock. As the young scholar nears college age, the percentage devoted to stock will gradually be reduced, which makes a lot of sense because the last thing you want is to lose a lot of money through a stock market implosion just before tuition bills arrive.

Safe Money Checklist

Putting Your Kids through College

✔ Apply for financial aid even if you don't think you have any chance of qualifying for it. Any financial aid will come in handy.

✔ If your financial situation deteriorates suddenly, consult with the college financial aid office about emergency loans and additional aid.

✔ It never hurts to ask the college for financial aid—or an increase in aid.

✔ Advance planning is always helpful, particularly for families with children who will be applying for college.

✔ College financial aid offices are ready to deal with the
financial crisis. With their help, you can be too.

✔ Avoid the risk of big losses in a 529 plan for a child
nearing college age by opting for the age-based
investment choice.

24 TIPS FOR WORRIED PRERETIREES

*We were doing all the right things to prepare for
retirement, and then, in a matter of a few weeks, we lost
the equivalent of the last seven years of retirement plan
contributions. It's so depressing. We're not sure we'll ever
be able to afford to retire.*

The worldwide economic meltdown has affected everyone,
but none so severely as retired people (see Chapter 25) and
preretirees—those who are within a decade or so of retirement.
It's no surprise that many preretirees have concluded that the
combination of severe stock market losses and the prospect or
reality of unemployment has seriously impeded their retirement
plans. This chapter will show various ways in which a worried
preretiree can move from despondency to renewed confidence
that he can achieve the kind of retirement that he had envi-
sioned. While your immediate concern may be recouping the
losses in your retirement nest egg, there are many other consid-
erations that will influence the kind of retirement you will enjoy.
They are discussed in this chapter. There *is* hope!

RECOUPING INVESTMENT LOSSES

The extent of your investment losses depends largely on the percentage of your money that has been invested in stocks. How you will fare in the future will also most likely depend on how you diversify your investments. Your most likely impulse—to get out of stocks altogether—will probably turn out to be the worst way to invest for retirement in the future.

While common wisdom suggests that the closer you get to retirement, the more conservatively you should invest, a more relevant consideration is how long you're going to need the money to last. Whether you're a year or a decade from retirement, you'll need your retirement money to last for decades, during which time your cost of living will double, if not triple. It's highly unlikely that retirement money that is invested solely in interest-earning securities will help you keep up with inflation throughout your retirement years unless you need to withdraw only a very low percentage from your retirement nest egg—no more than 2 to 3 percent. Most retirees need to withdraw more, and that's why they need the long-term growth potential of stocks for at least a portion of their retirement portfolio.

Part III covers the topic of investing, and the guidance given there applies just as much to preretirees as it does to people in other age groups.

While on the subject of investing, resist the temptation to lower the amount of money you're contributing to your retirement savings plans. While reducing the amount you put away during a market slump may seem to make sense, by forgoing your contributions, you're also forgoing current and future tax benefits. If you worry that the money you add will lose value, put it into something that won't lose value—a money market fund or stable value fund, for example.

"INVESTING" IN DEBT REDUCTION

In a time of great investment uncertainty, there are some "investments" that pay guaranteed returns. Paying down credit card, home equity, and mortgage loans reduces future interest charges, and over the years this can save you thousands, if not tens of thousands, of dollars in interest. For example, paying an extra $500 on a 19 percent credit card balance will have a 19 percent return, since you avoid paying interest on that amount in the future. If you can get your debt under control to the extent that you have paid it down or even eliminated it by the time you retire, your retirement prospects will be very much improved.

When it comes to mortgages, a little bit extra can go a long way toward paying it off sooner. Here's a case study of how adding to a mortgage payment can reduce the time it takes to pay it off. Celeste wants to retire in 10 years, and she has 15 years left on her $200,000 mortgage. She's surprised to discover that paying an extra $375 per month toward her mortgage will pay it off in 10 years, rather than 15. While that's a big bite out of her budget, if she can manage to make the extra payments, the amount of income she'll need during her first few years of retirement will be considerably lower if the mortgage is paid off.

FIGURING OUT HOW MUCH IT'S GOING TO COST YOU TO RETIRE

You may be pleasantly surprised to find out that it won't cost you as much to retire as you may think. Don't put too much credence in the usual rules of thumb that suggest you'll need a retirement income that's close to (some say in excess of) your preretirement income to live decently once you're retired. Everyone's situation is different, but many retirees have found that they can live quite well on 65 percent or less of their preretirement income. But it's up to you to figure out your own situation. To get you started on this exercise, the following table lists expense items that will probably decline after you retire. First, while you're still going to have to save a bit of your income in your early years of retirement, your need for savings will pretty much go away. Work-related expenses will also be eliminated, and, after decades of kicking money into social security, you'll be on the receiving end at last. Finally, your income taxes will decline, typically consuming about 10 percent less of your income. Of course, some expenses, notably medical costs, are likely to rise after you retire, but when you put pencil to paper, you're likely to find that you can enjoy a good retirement on less money than the pundits would have you believe. By the way, two other big expense items may also be eliminated or reduced by the time you retire: college and other child-related

Expense Reductions When You Retire

Expense Item	Spending Level
Savings	5 to 20%
Work expenses	3 to 5%
Social security taxes	6 to 8%
Expense reductions at retirement	14 to 33%
Reduced income taxes	10%
Expense and income tax reductions at retirement	24 to 43%

expenses, and the mortgage. If you're fortunate enough to eliminate those expenses, you're probably headed for an even more delectable retirement.

If you're still concerned about your retirement prospects, which the economic tsunami has definitely hurt, consider any of the following lifestyle changes that can turn a so-so retirement into a very prosperous retirement.

DECIDING WHERE TO RETIRE

Studies have indicated that many baby boomers intend to move after they retire—relocating in either the same locale (from city to suburbs or vice versa, for example), a different part of the country, or even a foreign country. You may be able to lower your retirement living expenses considerably if you decide to move to a less expensive locale. For example, moving to the Sunbelt from an urban location in the northeast or California can reduce your living expenses by as much as 40 percent.

DECIDING WHAT TO DO WITH YOUR HOME

Downsizing your living quarters either before or after retirement can be another helpful way to close the gap between the resources you have and the resources you need for retirement. Here are some of the potential financial benefits. The first is reduced debt in the event that you're likely to otherwise retire with a mortgage. Eliminating or reducing a mortgage that might erode your retirement budget could work wonders for your retirement living standard. Second, Uncle Sam rewards home sellers with a big break in capital gains taxes. Suffice it to say that you probably won't owe any federal income taxes when you sell your home unless you have a big-league gain on the sale. Furthermore, if your downsizing allows you to free up capital to invest, you'll enjoy more income throughout your retirement. Those who move into less expensive quarters also enjoy lower housing expenses—for example, property taxes and utilities. All in all, downsizing can result in a financial home run. You may also want to consider moving from being a homeowner to being a renter, which may allow you to get out from under a house that's dragging you down financially or use the equity in your home to help with retirement living expenses. You'll also avoid the hassles of being a homeowner when you have better things to do after you retire.

Deciding When to Retire

The age of retirement has a significant impact on lifetime retirement income.

Delaying Retirement

The following case study shows the difference between retiring early at age 62 and retiring six years later at 68. Betty has suffered some losses in her investments, but she estimates that she will have $300,000 in retirement savings at age 62. If she retires later, she will add $15,000 per year to her retirement savings through her retirement savings plan at work. If Betty retires at age 62, she'll have a total yearly income of $31,000, including social security and withdrawals from her retirement stash. But Betty is like most preretirees. She likes her job and sees no reason to leave the workforce at 62. On the other hand, Betty is wise to look at her situation in the event that she has to retire early. Over 40 percent of those who retire early do so involuntarily because of illness, caring for a family member, or, with increasing frequency, job loss. That's an eventuality that every preretiree should contemplate and plan for. But with any luck, Betty—and you—will have choices about when to retire. What a difference delaying retirement makes in the income Betty can enjoy. If she retires at age 68, rather than age 62, her first-year retirement income will rise from $31,000 to $57,000—an 84 percent increase! Also, she'll be able to increase her withdrawals to account for inflation each year for the rest of her life.

Retiring Gradually

Let's turn now to gradual or phased retirement, another approach that will be very popular with preretirees. Instead of retiring cold turkey, gradual retirees taper down their workweek. Once we get over the current bleak employment situation, part-time work will probably become more plentiful. American industry is apoplectic over the specter of experienced and dedicated baby boomers leaving the workforce. The following table shows what happens financially if you delay collecting social security and withdrawing money from your nest egg simply by earning enough money to support yourself without adding even another nickel to your savings. What a difference! For example, delaying retirement by three years will raise your social security check by 19 to 26 percent. The amount you can withdraw from your retirement wampum—for the rest of your life—rises about 25 percent.

The Benefits of Gradual Retirement

Increase in	Delay Retirement		
	1 Year	3 Years	5 Years
Social security	6–8%	19–26%	36–44%
Withdrawals from retirement nest egg	10%	25%	40%

Safe Money Checklist

Tips for Worried Preretirees

✔ Keep your investments well diversified so that you'll benefit from the stock market rebound.

✔ Reducing debt, including your mortgage, can save high interest charges and also improve your retirement prospects.

✔ Prepare an estimate of how much income you will need when you retire. It may be less than you think.

✔ Retiring in a lower-cost locale may reduce your retirement income needs.

✔ Downsizing your home can free up equity to add to your retirement nest egg.

✔ Delaying retirement or retiring gradually can improve your retirement prospects, perhaps significantly.

25 TIPS FOR WORRIED RETIREES

> *The economic disaster has me scared to death. Like most*
> *retirees, I can't afford huge losses in the stock market. But*
> *my investments keep dropping. Who knows what's going*
> *to happen to the economy? All I can say is that it looks*
> *like retired folks are taking it on the chin.*

A lot of media attention has focused on how the economy affects working people and businesses. Yet many retirees suffer even more from an economic downturn than other age groups.

- Most retirees live on incomes that are mostly fixed and that may actually decline during a recession, while living expenses continue to increase inexorably.
- Many retirees who rely on income from their investments to meet living expenses have found that those investments have been decimated by the turbulent stock and bond markets. It's like a "perfect storm." Stocks are way down, but interest rates paid by safe securities are also way down. In 2008, Treasury bill interest reached an all-time low, yet frightened investors flocked to Treasuries even though they were receiving almost no interest.
- The ever-present danger of rising inflation could thrust many retirees into a precarious financial position.

MAKING ENDS MEET

Does the following describe your situation as a retiree? You have always worried about your ability to meet the steadily increasing costs of living on a relatively fixed income, and the recent turmoil in the economy has heightened your concern. You don't have a luxurious lifestyle, and increases in the cost of many essentials are beginning to be a concern. As if this isn't bad enough, you've found that your investments, like everyone else's, have been performing miserably. Social security increases never quite seem to keep pace with inflation, and if you're fortunate enough to have a pension plan that is adjusted for inflation from time to time (at the discretion of the pension administrator), you suspect that future inflationary increases may be curtailed as governments and businesses look for ways to reduce spending.

If you are feeling squeezed, your situation is not very different from that of many working Americans. Therefore, you should be planning for the difficult times in much the same way that working-age people should. Even though you may not think that you can reduce your expenses, you probably can if you need to. Chapter 5 provides some guidance on preparing budgets for tough economic times, and Chapter 6 offers some tips if your expenses are rising faster than your income. If reducing your expenses is not enough, you may need to consider increasing your income. You may be pleasantly surprised to find that there are part-time work opportunities available for able-bodied retirees. Many companies that cut back on the number of full-time employees will be seeking lower-cost part-time help to perform needed tasks. So, don't just assume that because you are retired, you have no employment prospects. Start looking around, and consult your local or state council on aging or elder affairs department. AARP can also help retirees find gainful employment.

The keys to coping with the current financial malaise are to plan carefully; take reasonable, well-thought-out actions to meet your current and future financial needs; and avoid doing anything drastic to your finances without consulting with experienced and trustworthy professionals or family members first.

MANAGING YOUR INVESTMENTS

It's tough enough to manage your investments effectively at any age, but it's particularly tough during your retirement years. When you were younger, you could make some investment mistakes because you had many years to make up for them. Most retirees can't afford to make serious investment mistakes. Investing in the current environment is downright scary for retirees—and everyone else, for that matter. My feeling is that if you take a sensible, long-term approach to investing, you won't be affected too adversely during bad investment markets, and you will flourish during good investment markets, which will certainly return. Some general suggestions are given here. Refer also to Part III of this book, which discusses investing under the current difficult conditions. Take heed of the following recommendations whether you invest on your own or use an investment advisor. If you use an investment advisor, remember that it is *your* money and that you need to pay attention to how it is being managed. Unfortunately, many investment advisors, even those who work in big, well-respected institutions, have had a great deal of difficulty navigating the recent stock market implosion.

Invest for Growth as Well as Income

If you, like most retirees, rely on income from your personal investments to help pay your living expenses, some of these investments must also provide growth so that you can keep up with rising living costs. Stocks and real estate are the two investment categories that provide the most consistent, though erratic, inflation-beating returns. Many retirees feel that they should avoid these investments because they are risky. Certainly the performance of real estate and stocks during the recent world economic contraction amply illustrates the risk. On the other hand, over the long run, stocks and real estate have provided a much higher return than the third major category of investment, interest-earning securities like bonds and certificates of deposit (CDs).

This is not to suggest that you should go out and sell your CDs and buy a lot of stocks next week. On the other hand, although it is difficult to generalize, if a retiree's investment portfolio does not include any stock, it is likely to suffer from the erosive effects of inflation—not this year and not the next, but 10 and 20 years hence, when inflation will seriously diminish the purchasing power of investments that provide only income, like bonds and temporary investments like CDs. The fact is that retirees are living long and active lives today. Life expectancy tables indicate that a couple, both age 65, have a "last to die" life expectancy of 27 years. In other words, on average, one of them will live to age 92, and that is just the average. I hope that you will beat the average, but whatever happens, you will need to keep your eye on how inflation is going to affect you. You can't rely on your *income* to increase to keep up with inflation through annual raises as you did during your working years. Instead, you have to rely on your *investments* to grow with inflation, in addition to providing you with adequate interest and dividend income.

Maintain a Diversified Portfolio That Is Appropriate to Your Needs

As I discussed earlier, it's important that you have at least some inflation-beating investments in your portfolio, namely stocks. Real estate also provides that opportunity, but most retirees do not want to get involved in the hassle of owning individual properties, although you could—and should—invest in a real estate mutual fund. Excluding real estate, a balanced portfolio should consist of both interest-earning investments and stock investments. Generally, retirees should have a higher proportion of their savings invested in interest-earning investments than younger people would. But stocks still belong in most retirees' investment portfolios. Typically, retired investors should emphasize high-quality stocks with good dividend-paying records or mutual funds or exchange-traded funds that hold such stocks. High-quality stocks make particularly good sense in the current frightening stock market environment because well-established companies with the capacity to pay generous, regular dividends will not be as adversely affected by a declining market as other stocks.

As far as interest-earning investments are concerned, retirees who pay attention to the interest rates paid on various securities can be well rewarded, particularly when interest rates are quite low, as they are now. For example, a little comparison shopping among local banks or on the Internet is likely to uncover very attractive rates paid on FDIC-insured CDs. Finally, as in all areas of investing, spreading your money around among various types of interest-earning securities is the best solution.

Don't Do Anything Precipitous in Response to Market Uncertainty

Sometimes, retirees get themselves into financial trouble because they react too hastily to unfavorable investment market conditions. In other words, they may make a major change in their investments, often at the suggestion of some self-anointed expert. Certainly you need to be concerned about keeping your money safe amidst economic uncertainty and volatile investment markets. If you're so frightened that you want to concentrate more of your investments in safer securities, that's fine, but do so gradually. On the other hand, you may feel that you have invested too conservatively, or perhaps that stocks have been beaten down so badly that they are attractive. That's okay, too, but change your investments gradually over a period of months or even a year or two. That way, you won't suffer unduly if you guess wrong. And since most experts guess wrong most of the time, it is always possible that you may do so as well.

Don't Make Inappropriate Investments

Just as you have to maintain a balanced portfolio that consists of a variety of carefully selected investments made and monitored by you and/or your investment advisor, you also need to avoid making risky investments. Unfortunately, retired people are favorite targets for opportunistic or unethical salespeople who recommend overly risky or otherwise inappropriate investments. The best way to avoid making them is to stick with old-fashioned, plain-vanilla investments that you understand. If someone who is trying to sell you an investment can't describe it to your satisfaction in one sentence, don't buy it.

Be particularly careful of high-yield (high-interest) investments. Far too many seniors are burned in times of weak stock markets and low interest rates by being lured into investments that pay an unusually high rate of interest. Don't be a yield chaser. Opt instead for high-quality interest-earning investments. The current economic situation is hardly the time to invest your money in securities that pay unusually high returns. There is a reason why companies pay those returns, and it isn't because they like you a lot; it's because they are riskier. What good is earning high interest if you're going to lose your principal?

Keep Short-Term Money Safe

Retirees are understandably unhappy if they have to sell investments that have recently taken a drubbing to pay bills. It's better to give that money a chance to recover its losses. To avoid that unsavory situation, keep the equivalent of two years' worth of expenses invested in no-risk securities, like CDs and money market funds. This will provide at least some solace during a declining stock market, as you won't be compelled to "sell low" to pay your bills.

REVERSE MORTGAGES

If you are well into your retirement years and you own your home free and clear or almost free and clear, a reverse mortgage may help you offset lost income from the stock market decline. But you need to examine the ramifications of a reverse mortgage carefully.

A reverse mortgage is a loan based on the value of your home that you needn't repay until you move, sell your home, or die.

At your demise or when you move, the loan is repaid. In short, reverse mortgages can be an added source of income if you need cash and you have no heirs, or if your heirs are unconcerned about inheriting your home. (Even if they are concerned, it's your money and your life, so do what's best for you.) Unlike traditional loans, a reverse mortgage requires no income to qualify. But it generally comes with a host of fees, making it more expensive than a traditional mortgage. The longer you wait before doing a reverse mortgage, the more money you'll be able to get out of your home.

Matters to Consider

Reverse mortgages come in several flavors, including programs that pay you a lump sum rather than a lifetime monthly emolument, give you a credit line, or a combination of those. Be especially wary of any program that allows you to get all or most of the money up front. Receiving a large sum of money or a credit line may tempt you to use the money imprudently. It's far safer to opt for the monthly payment program. Carefully evaluate whether other options—such as selling your home—might prove more attractive. While you are probably attached to your home, comparing a reverse mortgage with selling your home and using the proceeds to buy or rent new quarters is the best way to evaluate whether a reverse mortgage makes sound financial sense. While the thought of moving from the family home may be anathema, you might welcome the possibility of moving into more manageable and less costly housing. If you have children, ask for their opinions as well. Finally, the permanence of a reverse mortgage should not be taken lightly. Too many things can happen during a long retirement, and the equity in your home is like an insurance policy. Tapping into it through a reverse mortgage is like cashing in a life insurance policy.

OTHER TIPS TO HELP YOU SURVIVE A SCARY ECONOMY

Maintain Your Insurance

If you begin to feel a financial pinch, you may be tempted to save money by dropping some of your insurance coverage, but this is penny-wise and pound-foolish. Always, *always* maintain your insurance coverage, particularly your health insurance. For persons 65 and over, this usually means keeping a Medigap insurance policy in force, which will protect you against incurring many large health-care bills. It is essential that you keep this coverage. Also, most retirees will benefit from Medicare Part D drug coverage. If you have a long-term care insurance policy, do your utmost to keep the coverage, even if the premiums increase.

Beware of Scam Artists

Sadly, seniors are all too often the victim of scam artists who will try to sell any number of services or investments to them. They are easy marks and are often too embarrassed to complain to anyone. There are two ways to avoid being taken. First, ask the salesperson to put whatever he is suggesting in writing. Second, mention that you need to check with a family member before making the purchase. Just telling the salesperson that you have to check with a relative before making a decision is enough to make most reprobates flee. We have a "$500 rule" in the Pond family. If parents are going to spend more than $500 on anything that someone else has suggested, they first check with one of the kids. This has worked very, very well.

Make Use of the Many Programs for Senior Citizens

Be sure to take advantage of any money-saving opportunities available to senior citizens in your local community and elsewhere. There are a great many valuable and money-saving programs, but it is up to you to uncover them.

A variety of organizations that represent retirees, including your local or state council on aging and the AARP, will be able to direct you to discounts.

Don't Hesitate to Seek Advice

Many retirees have been hurt by the Great Recession. If you become very troubled about your financial future, or if you are already experiencing financial problems, by all means seek the advice of qualified professionals or family members. They may be able to help allay your fears, provide a plan that will help you cope with your financial problems, or offer other needed guidance. How do you find experienced and trustworthy advisors? Don't go to the yellow pages or, worse, a "free" lunch. Ask your acquaintances or your family lawyer for a recommendation. As with all professionals, word-of-mouth referral is the best way to assure that you get the high-quality advice that you deserve.

Safe Money Checklist

Tips for Worried Retirees

✔ Evaluate how rising costs and declining investment markets will affect you over the next two years.

✔ If you find that you may have trouble making ends meet, start planning to take action that will help alleviate your financial strain.

✔ Maintain a diversified investment portfolio that includes appropriate portions of interest-earning investments to provide income and stock investments for the growth you'll need to meet rising living costs.

✔ Avoid making any quick, major changes in your investments.

✔ Be very wary of making any investments that are out of the mainstream or that you don't understand.

✔ Keep the money you will need over the next two years invested in safe securities.

✔ Carefully consider how a reverse mortgage might provide needed additional income.

✔ Always maintain your insurance coverage.

✔ Be on guard for scam artists; they're everywhere.

✔ Take advantage of cost-saving and service programs for retirees.

✔ Don't hesitate to seek the advice of family members or trustworthy professionals about your financial concerns.

26 SURVIVAL TACTICS FOR SMALL BUSINESS OWNERS

My friends who work for giant corporations are complaining about how the economic downturn is affecting their personal finances. I should be so fortunate.

My business is going through a terrible time. Sales are down, cash flow is weak, and the banks are hardly in a position to lend to us little guys. I've never experienced such a prolonged drop-off in business, and it looks as if the lousy business climate is going to continue for quite a while.

Small businesses are really struggling now. For every headline describing the travails of a major corporation, there are hundreds of small businesses that are on the brink. You need look no further than the large number of vacancies in downtown shopping areas and suburban strip malls in every region of the country.

A DOUBLE WHAMMY

Small business owners face a double whammy during an economic downturn. They have to keep both their business and their personal finances afloat. A big risk that small business owners face in a slowdown is that they will jeopardize their personal resources in an attempt to keep the business going. If that action fails, they could end up in serious financial trouble. Many business owners don't see their personal financial life as being separate from the business, even in the best of circumstances. When push comes to shove, they will gladly use their personal investments and retirement accounts, borrow against their homes, and cosign additional business loans to keep the business going. The risk of doing this is obvious, but small business owners are inherently risk takers anyway.

If you own a business or are a self-employed professional, the next section will discuss some strategies that may help you cope with the financial problems that plague many businesses and professions during a slowdown. It is followed by a discussion of the inevitable interrelationship between the finances of the business and the personal finances of its owner. If you are thinking about going into business for yourself, the concluding section offers some advice.

TAKING CARE OF BUSINESS

One key to dealing effectively with the recession's financial adversities is to anticipate problems and take action before it's too late.

Be Prepared to Take Action

Business conditions are already bad. Be prepared to respond quickly at the first sign of a slump by examining the effects of a slowdown on your business and outlining actions that should be taken under various possible slowdown scenarios.

Recognize Early Warning Signs

Don't wait for sales to slow down before taking action. Identify key indicators that are relevant to your business that will point to deteriorating or improving business conditions, so that you can take action at the earliest possible time. Critical indicators vary from business to business. The most obvious early warning sign is a slowing of sales. If your customers or clients are hurting, that will almost certainly reduce the amount of business they will do with you. Sudden changes in assets, such as increasing accounts receivable or inventories—or a decline in their turnover rates—may indicate impending problems. On the liability side, rising trade payables or short-term debt often signals trouble ahead. Using debt, even short-term borrowings, to support the day-to-day operations of the business is usually a bad sign, unless the business is seasonal. The inability to pass along increased costs to your customers suggests that demand is weakening, often an outcome of a recession or stronger competition. Either way, your company is likely to suffer a subsequent decline in sales. Keep in mind that your larger competitors have far more flexibility in reducing sales prices to their customers than you.

Don't Postpone Taking Corrective Action

Once you have determined that problems may crop up, take action immediately to address them. Business owners are an optimistic lot, and they may delude themselves into thinking that the problems will go away. You can bet that they won't, particularly during tough economic times. There are a number of things you can do to help weather a slowdown in your business.

If your business has inventory, reducing inventories is often one of the best ways to cope with slowing business conditions. Not only does a lower inventory tie up less cash, but it can also free up business credit lines, which can be used for other purposes if necessary.

Improving the management of accounts receivable is also an important means of keeping a business afloat. During a slowdown, your receivables will slow just like everyone else's, so you have to step up your collection efforts. If you're facing particularly tight times, this is no time to mollycoddle your customers. They will simply take advantage of you. On the other side of the balance sheet, avoid paying your accounts payable early, but don't stretch out payables too long, either. While delaying bill payments can help short-term cash flow, it will only aggravate the situation later on and could damage credit relationships. If extended payment terms can be arranged with some suppliers who may be anxious to prop up their own sales, take advantage of them.

Loans should, of course, be kept to a minimum during a slowdown. Highly leveraged companies, whether they are multi-billion-dollar corporations (case in point: the automobile manufacturers) or small businesses, are likely to falter, if not fail, during this recession. Alas, you can't count on a multibillion-dollar government bailout. If you get to the point where you are having difficulty meeting your loan obligations, much of the advice concerning consumer credit problems contained in Chapter 19 also applies to business indebtedness. Perhaps most important is keeping the bank informed of your problems and your plans to alleviate them.

If you haven't already, there are probably a number of areas where you can reduce expenses, particularly overhead, without adversely affecting your ability to do business. Approach layoffs with caution, unless you expect a lengthy slowdown. Layoffs by small businesses often impair the quality of the services or products those businesses are providing, not to mention the adverse effect on the morale of other employees. But if layoffs are necessary for the survival of the business, you have no choice.

If you are contemplating any major purchases for the business, you should consider whether it makes more sense to postpone them until you get a handle on how the recession ultimately will affect your business. On the other hand, you may find that, as larger companies curtail some of their products or services in response to the recession, you may have the opportunity to make inroads into other markets. This opportunity could justify some additional investment.

No matter how bad the situation gets, try to avoid becoming preoccupied with the survival of your business, lest it take crucial time away from the management of day-to-day operations. Build your employees into a team that is dedicated to fighting and conquering the adverse effects of the slowdown. You'll probably be pleasantly surprised at the extra effort they are willing to give.

SEPARATING BUSINESS FINANCES FROM PERSONAL FINANCES

As mentioned earlier, the biggest risk that you as a small business owner must confront in the face of deteriorating business conditions is not that you will lose the business; rather, it is that in losing the business, you also will wipe out your personal resources. If the prospects for your business are or become very bleak, you may have to make a very difficult decision—whether you should pour more personal resources into the business and/or cosign more loans to the business, assuming that you can get the loans at all, or whether you should cut your losses now. It is extremely difficult for most business owners to be objective and realistic about these matters. Only you can make that decision, but weigh carefully any action that could jeopardize your personal resources. It may not be worth it in the long run.

If you go through a business failure, remember that all is not lost. If you created a business once before, the odds are heavily in your favor that you can do it again. If you've had it with business ownership, take heart from the fact that many larger companies find former business owners to be superb employees, because they are highly motivated and have qualities that are lacking in many employees of large companies: the ability to think innovatively and address problems effectively. I have a good friend who was victimized by an earlier recession. He had spent a decade building up a large service business that collapsed in a matter of months. It wiped out all of his personal assets, including his home. Fortunately, he was blessed with a very supportive wife and children. After working for a company for about five years, and doing very well, he had the itch to strike out on his own again. He is now in the same line of business, but his organization is much leaner than his former, failed organization. I recently asked him how frightened he was of an economic collapse. He said that it didn't bother him a bit. His company is lean, and although business has slowed down, he now knows what it takes to keep his business going in slow times because, as he says, "I learned from all the mistakes I made a decade ago." Moreover, he now owns his home free and clear, and he has enough money in the bank to support the business for several years. His story is not at all unusual.

Is This a Good Time to Start a Business?

Economic crises often get people thinking about starting their own businesses. Millions of people have lost their jobs, and many millions more worry that they will be next. This makes the idea of working for yourself particularly attractive. Starting a business when conditions are weak may be efficacious. Since business is slow, you will have more time to devote to the necessities of building the business from scratch or buying a business. But if you decide to go out on your own, be sure your expectations are realistic. Don't expect to open a store, put a business online, hang out a shingle, and have people immediately knock down the doors, particularly in this moribund economy. Statistics have shown that it takes an average of seven years for a new business to become profitable. The most important first step is to find a business you'd love to run in a field where there is or probably soon will be strong demand and where you already have career experience (an affection for sushi doesn't qualify you to start a Japanese restaurant). You also need the money or the financial backing of partners to start and grow the business until it becomes profitable. This is not meant to discourage you from self-employment, but you have to approach it realistically.

Safe Money Checklist

How Small Business Owners Can Survive the Economic Crisis

- ✔ Be prepared to respond quickly at the first sign of a slump in business.
- ✔ Identify and monitor key indicators that will provide early warning signals of impending problems.
- ✔ If and when problems arise, take appropriate corrective action immediately.
- ✔ Avoid becoming preoccupied with the survival of the business at the expense of the management of day-to-day operations.
- ✔ Evaluate thoroughly and realistically the wisdom of committing additional personal resources to the business. You don't want to jeopardize your personal

investments and credit if the survival of the business is seriously in question.

✔ While starting or buying a business in a weak economy can be timely, consider the time commitment, cost, and risks of doing so.

27 THE PSYCHOLOGICAL SIDE OF MONEY PROBLEMS

There's been a lot of arguing around the house lately. I mean, it's normal to argue, but not as much as we are. Things have really been tough for the last year. I finally got another job after being out of work for six months. We didn't lose the house, but we are so far behind on our bills that any time anyone in the family mentions anything about money, the fur starts to fly. I even yelled at my son yesterday when he asked for some money so that he could go to the mall with his friends.

Everyone experiences money problems sometime during her life, and everyone argues with family members about money matters, but that's of little comfort if your family is going through financial problems now.

COMMUNICATION IS THE KEY

Sadly, money is so important to our self-esteem that money problems, even temporary money problems, can be devastating to us.

When confronted with money problems, we tend to withdraw at a time when we should be asking for help. We often spend too much time worrying about our problems and too little time working to address and resolve them. If there is one positive thing to say about financial problems, it is that they can be resolved. It may require a lot of work, it will probably require sacrifice, and it may well take a long time, but they can be resolved. One other thing is for certain, however: they won't be resolved as easily as they might be if you don't share your problems with others, including family members.

It all boils down to communication. Good communication is important to your financial health, not just with family members and close friends, but also with people who can help you with your financial problems. For example, Chapter 20 discusses what you should do if you fall behind or think you'll fall behind on your mortgage. The answer? *Communicate* with the lenders. Similarly, Chapter 19 deals with coping with anxious creditors and using credit counselors. The solution is not to avoid creditors' calls and letters. Instead, you need to *communicate* with them openly and honestly. Creditors have a vested interest in helping you resolve your credit problems, and many of them are particularly well prepared to assist you when conditions are particularly nettlesome because you're not alone in your problems.

But, oh, does pride get in the way! It's not easy to get on the phone soon after you have been laid off to tell your friends and professional colleagues that you are in the market for a new job. How do you think they'll react? Is it really that embarrassing? If a friend or colleague called you to tell you the same thing, how would you react? When adversity strikes, don't let pride get in the way of good sense. Use the many resources available to you.

YOU, YOUR MONEY PROBLEMS, AND YOUR FAMILY AND FRIENDS

Families survive financial crises. You've probably heard your parents or grandparents talk about the Great Depression. Families survived then. If you're going through your own great depression, you'll survive. It's as important to communicate openly with family members or close friends as it is with creditors, although you may feel that talking with creditors about your problems is easier than talking with family members. Generally, family members, including older children, should share in any sacrifices that will be necessary to resolve the problem. Even if there is no immediate crisis, you want to prepare for that eventuality during the recession; involve other family members in the planning and actions that must be taken. A spirit of cooperation will go a long way toward minimizing the family stress that inevitably accompanies a financial setback. If your money problems seem to be causing you or your family too much stress—and they may—by all means consult with a counselor.

Safe Money Checklist

Dealing with the Psychological Impact of Money Problems

✔ Seek the assistance and support of family members and friends if and when you experience financial problems. Resist the temptation to withhold this information from them.

✔ At the first sign of credit problems, contact your lenders so that you can work out a plan to repay the debt. Most lenders are prepared to work with you.

✔ Involve family members in developing and implementing plans to resolve financial problems.

28 BANKRUPTCY—THE LAST RESORT

Since my husband got laid off, we've had a lot of trouble paying our bills. Even the credit counselor can't work out a repayment schedule that our creditors can accept. I'm afraid we're going to have to declare bankruptcy, but I'm not sure what that entails. Will we lose everything?

Personal bankruptcies are already soaring, and since this crisis isn't going to go away very soon, the number of bankruptcy declarations is expected to rise, despite the 2005 changes in the bankruptcy laws that made filing for bankruptcy more difficult, more expensive, and more time-consuming. At least one million filings were made in 2008, with far more likely to be made in 2009 and subsequent years. If you anticipate credit problems, take all the steps described in Chapter 19 and work with a credit counselor to put yourself back into solvency. Consider bankruptcy only as a last resort. But when all else has failed, it may be your only alternative. A bankruptcy stays on your credit history and makes it difficult to get credit for up to 10 years, although many who have had to go this route have reestablished their good credit within just a few years.

On the bright side, declaring bankruptcy can get most of your debt problems solved and will halt any legal actions that lenders may have taken against you. Bankruptcy is a legal proceeding during which your responsibility for repaying certain debts is temporarily suspended while you and a bankruptcy trustee devise a plan for meeting as many of your credit obligations as possible. Your liability for certain debts may be limited to less than you owe, and other debts may be eliminated altogether.

Once a plan has been worked out, you repay your debts either from the forced sale of your assets or from your current income, depending on the plan.

If you are considering filing for bankruptcy, you will need to consult with a lawyer. Obviously, this isn't a great time to incur additional expenses, but you can seek free or inexpensive legal assistance, for example, through a local Legal Aid Society. Lawyers who specialize in bankruptcy may be inclined to push you to file, calling it an easy way out of your problems. Bankruptcy is not an easy way out, and should not be taken lightly.

TYPES OF BANKRUPTCY PROCEEDINGS

There are basically two kinds of bankruptcy proceedings available to you: Chapter 7, "straight bankruptcy," and Chapter 13, the "wage-earner plan." The type you choose will depend on your income, the type of property you own, and the amount and kind of debts you have.

- **Chapter 7.** Under Chapter 7, debts will be eliminated by a liquidation of the debtor's assets, so this is preferable if the debtor has few or no valuable assets to lose. In order to file under Chapter 7, the debtor must meet certain income requirements.
- **Chapter 13.** Chapter 13 is typically recommended for debtors who have fallen behind on their payments because of a temporary problem like a job loss, but who can get back on track if they are given some time to catch up. Bankruptcy under Chapter 13 generally carries less of a stigma than bankruptcy under Chapter 7.

WHAT'S PROTECTED FROM BANKRUPTCY?

You will not lose everything you own during bankruptcy proceedings, and debtors' jails have been abolished. If your debts are within certain limits and you have a steady job, you may be able to avert a forced sale altogether by filing Chapter 13. If you are required to file Chapter 7, you will be able to exempt certain assets from the sale, but the dollar limits for exempt assets are very low.

Under Chapter 13, the debtor is required to pay off all debts. Under Chapter 7, on the other hand, some but not all debts are discharged. Here are some of the debts that still have to be paid under Chapter 7:

- Certain back taxes and any fraudulent taxes
- Alimony
- Child-support payments
- Student loans, subject to certain conditions

EMERGING FROM BANKRUPTCY

While you may be credit-shy after undergoing a personal bankruptcy, you will need to rebuild your credit. First, get a new credit card. Initially, you may qualify only for a secured credit card—a regular credit card backed by a security deposit that you leave with the issuer. As far as qualifying for larger loans—a car loan or a mortgage—you won't have to wait the seven to ten years that the bankruptcy notation stays on your credit record. Most lenders want to see about a year's worth of on-time payments on various accounts, including utility bills. Nevertheless, even though you can obtain a car loan or a mortgage within a few years of filing, you'll probably be saddled with a higher interest rate, but you'll still be able to get back on your feet financially. Whatever your situation, whatever the forces that compel you to declare bankruptcy, the worst is over. Rebuilding your credit will take time and perseverance. But you will emerge and begin anew.

Safe Money Checklist

If You Are Considering Filing for Bankruptcy

✔ First try to work something out with your creditors to avoid filing for bankruptcy.

✔ Consult with a credit counselor and then an attorney.

✔ Familiarize yourself with the two types of bankruptcy proceedings, and, if you qualify for both, decide in conjunction with an attorney which one would be more advantageous to you.

✔ Determine whether enough of your debts would be discharged by bankruptcy proceedings to make this route worthwhile.

✔ Work hard to rebuild your creditworthiness when you emerge so that you won't repeat your credit problems.

29 IF INFLATION HEATS UP

I always thought that recessions meant prices would moderate, but now I am reading that the inflation rate is increasing. Does this mean that we're going to get a slowdown in business and lots of unemployment, with rising prices to boot? They say life is unfair, but how unfair can it get?

Simultaneous recession and inflation is not unheard of. It happened in 1973–1974 and again in 1981. Business was down, stock prices were declining, and prices of consumer goods soared. Some indicators are pointing to higher inflation, particularly if oil prices go back to the high levels of early 2008. Although higher inflation is far from a certainty, this chapter will highlight some tips that may help you if and when the inflation rate rises.

- If a period of higher inflation is likely, you should account for those costs in your budgeting, and make the necessary changes in your spending to reflect increased costs. While wages typically rise with inflation, there is always a lag between rising costs and rising wages. You should also consider the possibility that employers have been so badly hurt by the economic crisis that they will not be able to afford large raises even in the midst of rising inflation.
- If prices rise, so must your savings, because you will need more money set aside to meet the higher costs of whatever you will use your savings for, including coping with family financial emergencies and accumulating enough resources for retirement.
- Review your insurance coverage limits in light of higher inflation, particularly your homeowner's or renter's insurance policies. While some insurance companies automatically increase the limits of coverage each year to bring the protection into line with current costs, many do

not, and even those that do may not increase the limits sufficiently to account for higher inflation. This applies both to your home and to your personal possessions. Valuable possessions, in particular, may increase significantly during a period of high inflation.

- If you find that the costs of consumer goods are increasing rapidly, consider buying household necessities in bulk. But don't go overboard and spend money that you may need to help you through any tough times.

- You will hear a lot of people say that borrowing is a good thing to do during a period of high inflation, because you can repay these loans with "cheaper dollars." Many families have been ruined financially by taking that advice during earlier inflationary periods. The catch? They borrowed for silly reasons and didn't have any "cheaper dollars" around to repay their loans.

- If you have an adjustable-rate mortgage, and you expect that inflation will heat up and continue indefinitely, it may be time to switch to a fixed-rate mortgage. Check the provisions of your adjustable-rate mortgage to see how high the interest rate can go. While you may not be able to lock in a very attractive rate on a fixed-rate mortgage, it may be better than having to suffer from an even higher rate on your adjustable-rate mortgage.

- Inflation is a tremendous problem for any retiree whose income is wholly or partially fixed. Social security benefits rise with the cost of living, but many pensions and most annuities are fixed. Hence, retirees should have at least a portion of their personal retirement funds in investments that offer some hedge against inflation, notably stocks. Retirees also should save some of their income well into their retirement so that they will have sufficient resources to be able to cope with periodic high inflation later in life. See Chapter 25 for additional advice for retirees on coping with the uncertain economy.

- When inflation is high, so-called hard assets, such as a home, real estate, and precious metals, tend to do well, but this is not always the case. Bonds do rather poorly during an inflationary period because interest rates are pushed up. Thus, the value of older bonds that pay lower interest sinks, sometimes dramatically. A safe harbor during periods of high inflation is short-term investments, like money market funds and U.S. Treasury bills, whose interest rates tend to rise as inflation rises.

- Since real estate has generally been a good inflation hedge, a home becomes an even more attractive investment during a period of high inflation.

- In periods of high inflation, money invested in stocks is not as likely to lose its purchasing power as money invested in bonds that have a fixed maturity value.

- Don't fall for the hard-sell tactics that may be leveled at you by salespersons intent on protecting your home and hearth against the ravages of inflation. They want to sell you guaranteed inflation hedges, such as rare coins, gemstones, and gold bullion. If you take them up on their offer, the only guarantee is that you are going to be taken.

Part V

Planning for a Secure Financial Future

---

30 "Been Down So Long"— Getting Back on Your Feet

This crisis in the economy set us back quite a bit. Our investments are down, household expenses are rising, and our income is stagnant. But we're looking forward to getting back to where we were. Then we'll begin to improve our personal finances so that we will be better prepared for the future.

While the worldwide economic crisis has been the worst since the Great Depression, these unfortunate events do end. When we're going through them, however, we wonder if they ever will. We're probably in for a slow recovery after this catastrophe, so don't be surprised if there is some uncertainty as to what the economy will be like once the worst is behind us.

Once the economy starts to turn around, you should evaluate where you stand financially and begin to plan for better times ahead. (There is one exception to this: since the stock market reacts to future events, it will rebound before we see clearer sailing ahead.) Everyone has been hurt by this horrific recession, and many millions of families have been severely set back through unemployment, loss of a small business, bad investment performance, or other problems in making ends meet. Years, if not decades, of hard-earned savings have been decimated. Most of those who went into the turmoil loaded with debt will probably emerge from the recession loaded with debt. Whatever your circumstances, however, you can begin the process of rebuilding so that you will be able to look forward to a more secure financial future—one that will be better able to cope with the next recession, whenever it arises.

The following information will help you take action to get back on your feet.

REVIEW YOUR DEBT SITUATION

You may have been preoccupied with your tenuous loan situation during the recession, and now that matters are settling down, you probably would like to forget about your debts. That's not possible, of course, but at least your finances may have stabilized sufficiently to let you begin making progress on getting your loan balances reduced. This should be a high-priority item as you emerge from the doldrums. By all means, don't let the postrecession euphoria motivate you to add to your loan balances if they are still causing you problems.

IMPROVE YOUR CREDIT STANDING

Because so many millions of families went into this recession with too much debt, many will emerge with impaired credit ratings. If this applies to you, you should make an extra effort to ensure that you reestablish your good credit standing as soon as possible—not so that you can borrow yourself into trouble again, but rather to restore your ability to borrow in the event you need to in the future for worthwhile purposes or to meet financial emergencies.

RESTORE YOUR EMERGENCY FUND

If you, like many people, had to dip into your emergency fund and even your retirement funds to make ends meet during the bad times, restore your emergency fund to a level of at least three months' living expenses as soon as possible. If you didn't have an emergency fund in the first place, you may have seen how important it was as you struggled through the recession. Once your financial situation begins to improve, you can focus on building up your emergency fund. Getting into the habit of living beneath your means will help you cope with future financial reversals, while at the same time building up the money needed to achieve lifetime financial security.

EVALUATE POSTPONED EXPENSES

The financial strain of the recession may have caused you to postpone some necessary household expenses. If your financial situation has improved, review these items to see if it would be prudent to incur these expenses now. For example, if you postponed needed car repairs, home repairs, or appliance replacements, you may decide that now is the time to make the repairs or purchase the appliances.

BE REALISTIC

Getting back on your feet won't happen overnight. This is one of the frustrating things about personal finance. We can get into financial trouble in a matter of weeks or months, but it takes a lot longer to recover. Don't let financial recovery get you down. If you can make progress each day, whether it involves forgoing certain expenses, looking for ways to improve your job performance or earn outside income, or putting a few dollars in a savings account, you are on the road to recovery. And that progress, however small it might seem, will snowball.

DON'T REVERT TO YOUR OLD HABITS

Unfortunately, many people who have been adversely affected by the recession will struggle to get on their feet, only to revert to their old bad habits. Sadly, many people in this country are consigned to a lifetime of living hand to mouth. I am not talking about the impoverished; rather, I'm talking about middle-income and even high-income individuals and families. You know what your past financial experience has been. Do you really want to go back to your old ways, or is it time to make some progress so that you don't have to live in constant fear of creditors, or illness, or whatever other conditions might befall you? Do you really want to have to work the rest of your life? Believe me, it doesn't take that much effort to change your lifestyle so that you can turn the corner. You know that you should change, and there is no better time than now to begin to manage your finances more sensibly.

TREAT YOURSELF TO SOMETHING NICE

You've undoubtedly endured a lot during the recession. Times have been tough, family relationships were strained, and you may even have wondered whether you would survive. Well, you did, and I think that you should reward yourself and your loved ones by doing something that contradicts just about everything that I've asked you to do in this book. Go out and splurge. Take them to the most expensive restaurant in town—it probably could use the business right now—or spend a weekend at an expensive resort. Just don't put it on your credit card. Why do I suggest that you do something so financially frivolous? Because you survived the tough times. You deserve a treat.

31 HOW THE NEW ADMINISTRATION MAY AFFECT YOUR POCKETBOOK

M any people are saying that the recession could drag on like Chinese water torture. But the good news is that recessions often spark new investment opportunities. So it is with new presidential administrations. Everyone wants the inside scoop on what's going to happen and how to profit from it.

SPEND, SPEND, SPEND

You can expect Uncle Sam to spend what could be trillions of tax dollars to stimulate the economy. Exactly how the money will be spent is not entirely clear. Our government's structure is apt to trigger debate in Congress about whatever the president aims to do. Those who fear that one-party control of the White House and Congress could result in spending running amok should recognize that deep regional and ideological differences among Democrats on such matters as labor law, global warming, single-payer health care, the conduct of the wars, and the extent of the bailout, not to mention the inability to pay for such programs, are likely to mute bold initiatives, at least during the early years of the administration.

But given the pervasive economic problems, the Obama administration will look for ways to get the economy back on track. So long as the economy remains moribund, you can expect economic stimulus packages to get more money into the hands of taxpayers. Huge amounts are likely to be spent beefing up the country's infrastructure and creating jobs in the process. The government is likely to give money to the states to repair bridges, roads, railroads, and airports. Unemployment benefits may be extended further, so that people have more time to look for meaningful work. More financial aid will be devoted to health care at the state level. You may also see tax credits to help keep taxpayers' pocketbooks from running on empty. Also expect more direct help for homeowners so that they can modify their loan terms to prevent foreclosure.

Changes in the Tax Rules

Most observers anticipate an overhaul of the federal tax structure. But approval of major tax legislation in Congress would need the support of Republicans and some wavering Democrats. During the campaign, Obama promised a tax cut for the middle class, funded by tax hikes for those with incomes above $250,000. Be advised: the number one priority of both Democrats and Republicans is to get the economy back on track. So any tax cuts remain an uncertainty. Nevertheless, here's how Obama's tax plan would work, if and when it were enacted.

Higher Taxes on Investments

If you rack up investment profits, you're likely to pay more in capital gains taxes. Expect to see the long-term capital gains tax rate—for investments that you've held at least one year—rise to 20 percent from 15 percent. This means that if you have profits from stocks, bonds, mutual funds, or real estate held outside retirement accounts, it could pay to take those profits sooner—while you're being taxed at the lower rate.

The tax rate on dividends may also rise from 15 percent to 20 percent, which will make dividend-paying stocks at least a little less alluring.

Income and Estate Taxes

Most people expect that the Bush tax cuts, which are due to expire in 2010, will not be renewed. The timing of any tax reductions and tax hikes may be postponed if the economy remains on life support. But if and when they are enacted, high-income taxpayers can expect to see higher income taxes, maxing out at 39 percent, up from 35 percent under the old rules. Some have reported that higher tax rates could hit individuals earning $150,000 annually and $200,000 for married couples.

Also under consideration is a repeal or modification of the alternative minimum tax, which was originally designed to tax the rich who shelter a lot of money by taking advantage of the tax regulations. As a result of inflation, the alternative minimum tax also wound up hurting the upper middle class, so some relief may be in the cards.

The idea of abolishing the estate tax has probably died. This means higher estate taxes—at least for those who die in 2011 and beyond. How the new estate tax rates will take shape remains to be seen. But many people expect that estates under $3.5 million will not be taxed. So you can expect estate tax attorneys and insurance agents to be working overtime to help limit the tax bite for the wealthy.

As the tax change rumor mill goes into overdrive, keep in mind that it is folly to change your financial life in anticipation of what Congress and the White House might do. Until the final legislation is passed, we really have no idea what our elected officials are going to do for—or to—us. As the old saying goes, "The only two things in life that are certain are death and taxes, but at least death doesn't get worse every time the Congress convenes."

Investment Opportunities

The financial media love to speculate on ways in which investors can profit from a new administration. Here are some of the more sensible ideas that have been proffered.

Municipal Bonds

High-tax-bracket investors might want to start preparing now for higher taxes. Look to municipal bonds for attractive yields compared with taxable bonds. Tax-free bond rates are as high as those on U.S. Treasury bonds. Municipal bonds will be an even better deal in the event of a tax hike. Just be sure you invest in the highest-quality municipal bonds. Many states and municipalities are running large deficits as a result of the severe recession. So it pays to invest in the financially strongest states and municipalities. (See Chapter 12.)

Deferred Annuities

High-income investors also might consider tax-deferred annuities issued by the strongest insurance companies. Those are rated at least A+ by A.M. Best and AAA by Standard & Poor's. If there's a chance that you may need to withdraw early, you need to remember that annuities may come with surrender charges that last several years.

Stock Sectors

Industries that are expected to do well during the Obama administration include

- **Alternative energy.** Alternative energy development should benefit, with increased emphasis on getting away from oil dependence. But investments in alternative energy, such as wind, solar power, and clean coal technology, could take years to bear fruit, since these technologies are still in the early stages of development. Two areas that may provide more immediate opportunities are natural gas and ethanol. Utilities are expected to use more natural gas to meet electricity demand; ethanol is already being used, and demand for it is likely to increase.
- **Health care.** Changes in the health-care system are anticipated, but no one knows for sure when or if a

national health-care system will debut. Some health-care sectors may benefit, while others could be hurt. Analysts say that giving millions of uninsured persons health-care coverage would cut health insurance company profits. But hospitals may benefit, since broader coverage will reduce one of the biggest drags on hospital profits: paying for uninsured patients. Companies engaged in stem cell research and preventive health care also may do well under this administration.

- **Infrastructure.** Massive amounts of money are likely to be provided for repairing the nation's infrastructure, notably bridges, roads, tunnels, and public transit. Many construction companies and their suppliers could benefit from this spending.

Buyer Beware

While speculation about investment opportunities under the new administration abounds, don't bet the ranch on supposed opportunities or flee stocks that the pundits expect will fare poorly under the Democrats, such as defense and drug companies. The depth and length of the worldwide economic crisis are likely to delay, if not negate, the initiatives that were ballyhooed during the campaign.

For What It's Worth Department

How will all the contemplated tax law changes affect the stock market? Historically, it pays to be optimistic. The average return on stocks when taxes rose by at least 10 percent was 16 percent in the year of the tax increase. The only period in which the stock market dropped during a tax hike was during the Great

Depression of the 1930s. Here's another tidbit for those who follow history: the stock market tends to do better under Democratic presidents, albeit only slightly better.

32 PROFITING FROM PROSPERITY

We have covered myriad topics, ranging from the unpleasant to the downright depressing. Tough times are tough on people. If you have had to suffer during the bad times, you certainly deserve to prosper during the good times. A few tips that may help you on your way to well-deserved prosperity follow.

1. **Prepare for a slow recovery.** Unlike previous recessions, this one is so deep and so wide-ranging that the hangover effects are likely to be felt for years. But as conditions improve, so will your confidence that you can get back on a firmer financial footing. Incidentally, if you're looking for a single signal that we're turning a positive corner, signs that the real estate market is on the mend could be it. We are suffering from both an economic crisis and a crisis of confidence. Once we start to see real estate prices in our communities rising and mortgage money becoming more available, our confidence in the future should revive.

2. **Readjust your investments to reflect new market conditions.** The investment strategies that were outlined in Part III emphasized defensive investing. As the

economy begins to improve, you may want to readjust your investments away from a defensive strategy to a more aggressive strategy. Be bold, but be prudent. For example, you may want to gradually increase the proportion of your money that is invested in stocks, even though you may now think that stocks are a one-way ticket to financial perdition. The outlook for real estate will also improve, so you might consider real estate investments as well.

3. **Tune in to new opportunities.** You have probably spent a lot of time worrying about the economic tsunami. In due course, you won't have to spend your time worrying about a recession, at least until the next recession comes along. Spend that time dwelling on a more satisfying subject: looking for ways to profit from rapidly evolving trends and improving world conditions. Some things that come to mind include our aging population, environmental concerns, the rapid growth of many foreign economies, and further technological advances of yet unknown proportions.

4. **Look for opportunities to advance in your career.** Perhaps you lost your job during the recession and took another one that is far from ideal. As the economy begins to pick up steam, you may find that an opportunity for a better job will open up. If you are happy where you are, begin to plan how you will advance at your place of work. The single best way to improve your financial situation is to have a steadily rising income that exceeds the rate of inflation. So if you can advance in your career, and thereby earn more income while keeping your expenses under control, you'll be in fat city.

5. **Participate in retirement plans.** As most Americans struggled through the recession, retirement planning took a backseat. Our attention was focused on more pressing matters. But preparing for retirement is one of the most crucial tasks for all working-age people. Now that you are back on a firmer financial footing, review where you stand with respect to achieving a great retirement. Ideally, you should be participating to the maximum in any company-sponsored plans, such as 401(k) and 403(b) plans. Consider contributing to an IRA each year as well. If you had to cut back on your plan contributions, strive to get back to your former contribution level. If you had to reduce or withdraw your plan contributions or if you're just starting out, the best way to get back on track is to do so gradually. Start with a level you can easily afford and work up from there.

Don't Let Pervasive Pessimism Cloud Your Good Judgment

In the first chapter, I chronicled the awful financial headlines that appeared in a single day in late 2008. It was enough to spur people into sticking their money into the proverbial mattress. But before you hollow out the mattress, consider another list of unhappy events during a previous period of maximum pessimism. I dusted off some old files, and found the following events that happened in a single day in 1990:

- Stocks and bonds both weakened significantly.
- Ford increased its loan loss reserves at its big financial subsidiary.

- General Motors announced that it was going to idle at least 11 U.S. assembly plants, amid weakening sales.
- Chrysler posted a $214 million quarterly loss.
- World oil prices rose.
- Airlines announced fare boosts to counter falling profits.
- A major consulting company laid off 17 percent of its employees.
- Employee-benefits experts indicated that early-retirement incentive plans appeared to be losing favor as an alternative to outright firings.

If this sounds familiar, you're right. These headlines are not very different from those appearing in Chapter 1. But let's go back to 1990 for a moment. Was the news bad enough to make investors flee the stock market? You bet. And the bad news continued into 1991. But here's what happened to the stock market (as measured by the Standard & Poor's 500 Stock Index) in the years after 1990:

1991	+ 31%
1992	+ 8%
1991–2000	+401%

That last number is not a typo. For the decade from 1991 to 2000, stocks rose just over 400 percent. For centuries, savvy investors have profited from either staying invested or adding to their investments when pessimism is rampant. In the early nineteenth century, British financier Baron Nathan Rothschild said: "The time to buy is when blood is running in the streets." That sentiment has not changed. Almost 200 years later, Warren Buffett said: "Be greedy when others are fearful and fearful when others are greedy."

We've come a long way. My greatest hope is that you will begin to take *some* action to help you through the Great Recession, so that you can take advantage of the prosperity that will inevitably follow. Do take some action. You'll like the feeling, and pretty soon not only will you be recession-proof, but also, and more important, you'll be well on your way to achieving financial peace of mind. Good luck!

Appendix: Web Sites to Help You in Tough Times

The Internet can be a great source of financial guidance and information, but the vast number of sites available can be overwhelming. The following sites will help you navigate the maze so that you can take advantage of the many ways in which the Web can help you in tough times. Since many of the following Web addresses are quite extensive, the special reader Web resource www.jonathanpond.com/safemoney.html contains hot links to these sites so that you can access them without having to type in the address.

Chapter 5, "Budgeting for Tough Economic Times"

Retirement Projections

Everyone should periodically prepare a projection of his retirement income and expenses. It's a hassle, but less so if you use the Web for guidance and to help with the number crunching. Some sites that are useful for this are

- www.analyzenow.com
- www.choosetosave.org/ballpark/
- www.finance.cch.com/text/c40s05d160.asp
- www.office.microsoft.com/en-us/templates/
  TC010421091033.aspx
- www.usaaedfoundation.org/financial/re08.asp

Household Budgeting

Here are some Web sites that provide either downloadable or fill-in-the-blanks budget worksheets. They each eliminate a lot of the drudgery involved in setting up and monitoring a household budget.

- www.bankrate.com/msn/news/debt/debtguide2004/home-budget-tool1.asp
- www.aarp.org/money/financial_planning/sessionthree/budgeting_and_record_keeping.html
- www.free-financial-advice.net/create-budget.html
- www11.ingretirementplans.com/webcalc/jsp/ws/determineHouseholdBudget.jsp
- www.extension.oregonstate.edu/catalog/pdf/ec/ec1302.pdf

Household Inventory

It's wise to maintain an inventory of your household possessions in case disaster strikes. The following Web sites will help you:

- www.jonathanpond.com/householdinventoryworksheet.html
- www.knowyourstuff.org

CHAPTER 6, "WHAT TO DO WHEN YOUR EXPENSES ARE INCREASING FASTER THAN YOUR INCOME"

Here are some coupon Web sites that will save you money if you shop in stores or on the Internet.

- www.dealhunting.com
- www.ebates.com
- www.thecouponmom.com

CHAPTER 7, "GETTING YOUR DEBTS UNDER CONTROL"

Switch credit cards if you can find a better interest rate. Card-Trak is a publication that spotlights the best rates on credit cards:

- www.cardtrak.com

To order free annual credit reports:
- www.annualcreditreport.com

CHAPTER 8, "FOREWARNED IS FOREARMED— PREPARING FOR THE UNEXPECTED"

Federal Insurance for Bank and Credit Union Deposits
To find out about FDIC insurance coverage for bank deposits:

- www.fdic.gov

To find out about credit union insurance for credit union deposits:

- www.ncua.gov/ShareInsurance/index.htm

CHAPTER 9, "INVESTMENT STRATEGIES FOR FRIGHTENED INVESTORS," AND CHAPTER 10, "TEN RULES FOR INVESTING SUCCESSFULLY IN TURBULENT MARKETS"

To learn more about investing so that you can better cope with the Fear Economy:

- www.aaii.com
- www.beginnersinvest.about.com
- www.easyallocator.com

- www.fool.com
- www.invest-faq.com
- www.investopedia.com
- www.investorhome.com/mutual.htm
- www.mfea.com
- www.rothira.com
- www.sec.gov (under "Investor Information," click on "Publications")

For education on mutual fund investing:

- www.morningstar.com

For mutual fund ratings and alerts:

- www.fundalarm.com
- www.reuters.com (click on "Markets" in the left column, then click on "Funds" in the left column)

For guidance on automatic investing:

- www.mfea.com (click on "Getting Started," then on "The Basics," then on "The Power of Automatic Investing")
- www.dripadvisor.com
- www.sec.gov/answers/drip.htm

For top yields on CDs and other safe investments:

- www.bankrate.com

For guidance on the advantages and drawbacks of annuities:

- www.businessweek.com/magazine/content/ 05_30/b3944410.htm

- www.chicagotribune.com/business/yourmoney/
  sns-yourmoney-0723cruz,1,3842886.story
- www.immediateannuities.com/

CHAPTER 13, "MAKING THE RIGHT REAL ESTATE INVESTMENTS"

If you're ever about to be smitten by somebody's can't-lose real estate investment strategy, check out John Reed's Web site. This newsletter author offers evaluations and recommendations of an extensive list of real estate gurus.

- www.johntreed.com/realestate.html

CHAPTER 15, "IF YOU LOSE YOUR JOB"

These sites will help you in your job search:

- www.careerbuilder.com
- www.monster.com
- www.glassdoor.com

CHAPTER 16, "IF YOU THINK YOU MIGHT LOSE YOUR JOB"

These sites will provide guidance for those considering a career change:

- www.careerjournal.com
- www.hotjobs.yahoo.com/careerchange

The U.S. Department of Labor–sponsored Web site, "Career One Stop," contains a plethora of useful guidance, diagnostic tools, and Web links to help you advance in your career or change careers:

- www.careeronestop.org

CHAPTER 19, "COPING WITH DEBT PROBLEMS"

Information on debt management and consumer protection:

- www.bankrate.com (click on "News & Advice," then on "Debt Management")
- Federal Trade Commission, www.ftc.gov (click on "Consumer Protection," then on "Consumer Information," then on "Credit & Loans."

Information on credit counseling:

- U.S. Department of Justice, www.usdoj.gov (type "credit counseling" into the search box, first article in stack)

To find a legitimate credit counselor:

- National Foundation of Credit Counseling, www.nfcc.org

CHAPTER 20, "ADVICE FOR HOMEOWNERS"

If you're having trouble paying your mortgage:

- www.hud.gov/

CHAPTER 22, "OPPORTUNITIES FOR HOME BUYERS"

Checklists for purchasing a home:

- www.mortgageguide101.com (click on "Home Buyer Checklist," second to last item in left-hand column)
- www.hud.gov/buying/checklist.pdf

To shop for low mortgage rates:

- www.bankrate.com

CHAPTER 23, "GETTING THE KIDS THROUGH COLLEGE"

- www.360financialliteracy.org/Financial+Topics/ Education+Planning/Articles/529+plans/529+Plans+ vs.+Other+College+Savings+Options.htm
- www.collegeanswer.com/index.jsp
- www.collegeboard.com
- www.finaid.org

CHAPTER 24, "TIPS FOR WORRIED PRERETIREES"

For articles on how the tough economy is affecting those planning for retirement, visit www.aarp.org and click on "Money."
Understanding your social security benefits:

- www.ssa.gov
- www.ssa.gov/estimator
- www.ssa.gov/mystatement/

- www.ssa.gov/planners/calculators.htm

Retirement planning information and guidance:

- www.worklife.state.ny.us/preretirement/selfhelpguide/

CHAPTER 25, "TIPS FOR WORRIED RETIREES"

For articles on how the economy is affecting retirees, visit www.aarp.org and click on "Money."
Reverse mortgages:

- www.aarp.org (click on "Money and Work," then on "Reverse Mortgages")
- www.reversemortgage.org
- www.hud.gov/offices/hsg/sfh/hecm/rmtopten.cfm

CHAPTER 26, "SURVIVAL TACTICS FOR SMALL BUSINESS OWNERS"

- www.cch.com (click on "Business Owners Toolkit")
- www.entrepreneur.com
- www.inc.com
- www.sba.gov
- www.score.org

CHAPTER 28, "BANKRUPTCY—THE LAST RESORT"

- www.bankruptcyinformation.com

OTHER SITES

For Jonathan Pond's columns, videos, advice, and commentary:

- www.AARP.org (search for "Jonathan Pond")
- www.SBLI.com

Visit the special *Safe Money in Tough Times* reader Web site for additional Web sites that will help you survive the Great Recession:

- www.jonathanpond.com/safemoney.html

SPECIAL READER OFFERS

If you would like trustworthy and timely information on important matters to help you keep your investments and personal finances in order, you can take advantage of the following special offers and discounts:

- Discounts on Jonathan's products and services, including his weekly Smart Money Tips and flash reports
- Newsletter offers
- An invitation to become a member of Jonathan's Financial Freedom Alliance

To find out more and to be kept informed of special reader offers in the future, visit www.jonathanpond.com/specialoffers.html.

INDEX

ABOUT THE AUTHOR

Jonathan D. Pond is an Emmy Award-contributor and host of 18 prime-time public television specials about investing and personal finance. He appears regularly on network and cable television stations and is a guest on radio programs throughout the country. Pond is the recipient of many awards, including the Malcolm Forbes Public Awareness Award for Excellence in Advancing Financial Understanding.